Leadership Is—

How to Build Your Legacy

A Business Life Investment Model

Glen Aubrey

www.ctrg.com

Creative
Team
Publishing

Creative Team Publishing
San Diego

First printing of the edition published by Creative Team Publishing.

Permissions and Credits:

Quotations from edition of *Essays: First Series* (1841) by Ralph Waldo Emerson used by permission of http://www.emersoncentral.com.

Scripture taken from the *Holy Bible, New International Version*. Copyright 1973, 1978, 1984 International Bible Society. Used by permission of Zondervan Bible Publishers. All rights reserved.

Scripture taken from *The Holy Bible, King James Version*. Copyright 2000 by the Zondervan Corporation. All rights reserved.

Song lyrics from "Love To Be Love" by David Hopkins, Copyright 1970, used by permission of Lisa Hopkins.

ISBN: 978-0-9838919-8-7
PUBLISHED BY CREATIVE TEAM PUBLISHING
www.CreativeTeamPublishing.com
San Diego

Printed in the United States of America

Leadership Is—

How to Build Your Legacy

A Business Life Investment Model

Glen Aubrey

You are more important than what you do.

The worth of what you do comes from
the person you are and the core values you embrace.

Table of Contents

Leadership Is— Introduction

"Leadership" is a term representing an expanding collection of paradigms, formulas and practices. Up-to-the-minute "How to Lead" method books appear on booksellers' shelves and websites regularly. It's a hot topic. Public consumption of information about leadership grows unabated. How many new leadership guides have you or your organization read lately? So consider, how much real leadership is being produced and practiced in the current business world as a result of the assimilation of these most recent views? The answer, of course, depends on what is meant by "real leadership."

Within these pages, a foundation for leadership structure and implementation will be built based on timeless principles and timely application. You are invited to determine if the leadership ideals and ideas take hold of you, if you agree with the premise and practices, and if you would be willing to put these into action. Principles when followed change people's behavior; indeed, life-engagement is affected, producing enduring results for the leader and those whom the leader impacts.

You've probably seen televised "extreme sports." Get a visual on this: half-pipes, skateboarders' limber frames turning, rolling, dipping, rising and falling seemingly without regard to gravity, of the situation or the physics. Across the bottom of the TV screen scrolls this message (repeated for emphasis): "Don't try this at home." "Don't try this at home." "Don't try this at home." Even with protective gear, it is high-risk activity with a goal of perfection.

Leadership, too, can be high risk; however, not with a goal of perfection, rather, perseverance. You can try what you read here at home; in fact, you are strongly encouraged to. Take the risk of leading well. Leadership based on principles endures, because principles endure. Embodied in their very natures are encouragements to utilize them in all of life's arenas repeatedly. Principles applied at work will affect community, home, and family. Balance in one will be evidenced in efforts to achieve balance in others because principles are transferable. Actively try to apply what you learn: at work, with your project team, your club, at the gym, playing sports, at home, on the golf course, in the sewing group, at school, wherever you are among people who may look to you for leadership's example.

The title phrase is a play on its words, of course. "Leadership Is—" means first that it exists, and because it exists and may be desired, we will deal with it. The phrase also constitutes an unfinished sentence. The student of leadership completes this sentence in ways he or she chooses. This same student considers numerous opinions and scores of options gleaned from a plethora of books, seminars and "leadership gurus" who all possess a theory of what leadership should be. *Leadership Is—* is an additional offering, a small one in comparison to some, perhaps one from which you may profit even more. Let's see.

If you are "in charge" of anything or anyone, the question isn't whether you are leading, the question is what kind of leadership you are choosing in front of those who look to you. Right from the outset, the leader has to decide: *what degree of personal choice and responsibility helps contribute to a follower's success?*

When they look carefully, leaders discover that few "new" leadership models are appropriate and worthy of exercise from a personal investment point of view; the faster and more competitively paced environments in which business is conducted discourage taking time for people. But leaders also learn that building into people has some great rewards.

> Investment in the follower is the central nugget of truth in leadership that works and builds legacies that last.

Investment in the follower is the central nugget of truth in leadership that works and builds legacies that last. Great leadership is robbed of its core of integrity and potential for positive change when a practicing leader does not act upon the essential truth of building into the people that follow.

Success in leadership achievement is defined as seeing another person fulfill their dreams and goals with the leader's teaching, modeling, encouragement and support.

Success in leadership achievement is defined as seeing another person fulfill their dreams and goals with the leader's teaching, modeling, encouragement and support.

Leadership implies followers, and in the course of leading people, those who are in positions of authority and influence are called upon to responsibly choose the types of people investment in which they will engage themselves and the people they impact. In a healthy leader-follower environment, the follower witnesses and duplicates the examples shown from the leader, and because principled actions are transferable, invests these into another follower, guaranteeing legacy. Followers carry on what leaders have modeled when the followers emulate their leaders, not because they have to, rather, because they want to. Creating earnest desires to emulate well builds ownership and leadership-transfer that transcends circumstance, and builds character: a worthy goal.

The lasting and positive choices of engaged leadership

build tracks of networking in which relationships of Dependence (Impact Leadership), Independence (Influence Leadership), and Inter-Dependence (Investment Leadership), are created and modeled (see Chapter 2). Leadership choices set the tone and provide the context in which healthy relationships are born and flourish, or in which seeds of unhealthy relationships, where trust and accountability are virtually or actually absent and improper ownership and selfishness become the rule and not the exception, are planted and nourished. Consequences of investment in followers' lives are consistent with and integrated into a leader's deliberate choices of the kinds of leadership to be employed.

Leadership is a decision, one that not everyone can or will make, and it may be a gift or calling as well. Defined: leadership is a state of interaction with others that can and must be cultivated to create duplicative results for positive and regenerating impact. Followers look to leaders to provide examples of how to follow as well as lead. That truth simply adds more importance to leading and following well, where following and leading are patterned according to a regenerating model where character and consistency are the motivators.

Effective leadership should not and does not die with the leader. Leadership that is lived out changes lives, and looks continuously for ways to expand roles of accomplishment through dedicated followers, regardless of the tasks, who so own the leader's principled and applied investment that their impact becomes even stronger in the leader's absence. The result is duplication that is both truth sustaining and life enduring.

> Leadership is a state of interaction with others that can and must be cultivated to create duplicative results for positive and regenerating impact.

Reducing leadership to a set of laws, forms or formulas may represent efforts to simplify what is really not that simple. It is responsible and right to position leadership as an attribute of character development that may be evidenced in multiple styles of presentation through varied personalities. This view sees great leadership as a result of intentional choice, building its foundation based on principles that shall not change even though the leader's methods of its application might. This view is not simple, but it is significant and worth the pursuit to understand it, and do leadership well.

The contents that follow are built upon solid and unalterable leadership precepts of life-giving, life-sustaining service—an immutable standard. In this examination, we will explore *Who Leaders Are and What Leaders Do—The Principle of Life-Investment, Leadership Tracks and Traits, Investment Leadership Initiative, Qualifying Trials, Quality Investments, Quantifying Tests, Creating Leadership Models that Work, Moving People, Leadership's Finish: Lines of Success,* and *Action Steps.*

Leadership Is— contains a selection of case studies entitled "Living Proofs." Living Proofs are illustrative stories from actual incidents. The incidents showcased and the principles applied occurred through real people in real work environments. Names and business enterprises of companies are fictitious; names of real participants have been changed. Any resemblance to actual names of people or situations within recognizable companies is purely coincidental.

Living Proofs are placed throughout the book to show what real-life applications of principles presented in *Leadership Is—* can be, as changes in behavior bring about good consequences. These consequences are proofs that leadership based on principle can build legacies that last.

When a company VP asked a leadership consultant from Creative Team Resources Group, Inc., (http://www.ctrg.com) whether or not the consultant could guarantee that his product would work if purchased for the VP's company, the consultant replied with a smile, "Absolutely not." When questioned why, the consultant responded, "Because I am not in charge of your character." Existing character and determination a leader brings to the table will make up a grid of understanding and application that within that leader's own experience may or may not bring about the success the leader may desire. That leader may have to change his or her perspective and behavior first if change in an organization is to come to pass.

When a leader sees that change is needful—in his or her character and habits—in a work group, a family, any environment, the leader quickly concludes that causing that change to occur can be tough. Guarantees of human participation are difficult, if not impossible, to manufacture or force. If change is needed, attitudes have to open up and be receptive; character needs to be exposed. Imposed change contradicts inclusive change, and inclusive change is preferred. Real desires for change are built through giving and receiving great information that encourages investigation on the part of those who need to change, because they see the benefits and then want them earnestly enough to make the efforts needed to achieve them. Learning becomes living, and communication is completed when behaviors change willfully, because the ones who need to change own the process. That's the goal.

If you are the leader, use the Living Proofs as encouragements toward quality decisions and changes you will be called upon to consider as you read. You will see that change is going to begin with you before beginning with those you lead. When you change, you initiate constructing your legacy through the others who follow you, because they view your example and want to emulate it. If you agree with what is presented, *you* will act. You will choose a leadership track and methodology that best suits you and those you lead. Lives will be affected, and your experience will likely become its own living proof within your spheres of impact, influence, or investment. Build your legacy.

Enjoy the run.

1
Who Leaders Are and What Leaders Do—
The Principle of Life-Investment

Fundamental to the core of people development is this truth: People are more important than what they do, and relationships precede and give definition to function. If you were convinced that you were more important than what you do, who would benefit? And, who does the convincing?

If you were convinced that you were more important than what you do, who would benefit? And, who does the convincing?

While the premise may be easy to state, the decision to acknowledge and apply its truth causes behavioral change, and change can be uncomfortable. The benefits far outweigh the discomfort, however, everyone benefits from acceptance and application of the principle over time. The individual does his or her own convincing, and the convincing moment occurs when intangible traits of solid character become more sought-after than temporary and tangible acquisitions.

> People are more important than what they do, and relationships precede and give definition to function.

The term "Relationship" is defined as the decision one makes about another's success. The term "Function" is defined as the real-life corroboration of the decision. Within relationships reside the seeds of a person's inherent worth, the development of value systems of belief, and the framework for choices about right and wrong. Function (what a person does) becomes the evidence of the quality of the decisions made.

If you should desire to be a values-driven leader, you will recognize and embrace this truth: The worth of a person is not determined first by his or her external contributions, rather, by the internal decisions about what is right. Further, individual decisions about the significance of people lead to the choices a leader makes about supporting follower's successes. "People are more important than what they do" puts relationships as primary over function. It does not mean a denial of the merit of production. Alternatively, it aligns the person and the function correctly. What a person does is determined by who a person is. Worth is inherent within the person first and the performance second. The marriage between relationship and function occurs naturally, the two are never separated; one gives birth and credence to the other.

A leader will understand and incorporate character choices, the intangible core values both leader and follower share in agreement and upon which they decide to act. These mutual core values, born in relationship, constitute the reasons for decisions about how to support another's success, provide the basis, and become the motives behind the methods a leader and follower employ.

The leader, for longer than today, views leadership from a person-value perspective and sees the long-term benefits to building the person and through the person building his or her contributions. If dedicated effort is expended in building functional output exclusively, the result may be sufficient output, but often at the cost of the provider. When a leader builds into a follower and through the follower generates greater output, the win is double: greater people and greater production. Simple math tells us that this is preferable. However, leadership that builds people first generally consumes more time up front, is more costly, higher-risk, but in the right time and place and with the right person, worth every effort. Clearly this kind of leadership requires a dedication to shared values that far exceeds the tendency to bend to circumstance, expediency or mere convenience "just to get the job done." Ends here do not justify means; in fact, the process here is more important than the product.

When choosing to lead, a leader earnestly seeks to commit to the highest principled life investment in light of the greatest benefits desired. Perhaps you will commit to this.

Results of great investments are seen in follower's lives, making the choices surrounding the investments most important: the choices of whom, what, when, why, where and how. The quality of the investment is built upon shared core values of belief, nurtured from the heart of the investor, and determines the quality of the return. Leaders, therefore, will weigh their investment roles and responsibilities carefully.

Who Is a Leader and What Does a Leader Do?

- Leaders are believers in people investment who understand the roles and responsibilities that accompany authority.
- Leaders learn to follow first, recognizing that followers look to leaders to learn how to follow before they look to leaders to learn how to lead.
- Leaders share core values in agreement with those who follow.
- Leaders are examples of ultimate expressions of integrity and high moral character at the cores of their being.
- Leaders are people-oriented, possessing service

attitudes to promote unity of relationship and function.

- Leaders dedicate themselves to people investment and excellence of function, in that order.
- Leaders set the pace because they create it.
- Leaders talk less and listen more, encourage others to speak, request advice and input more than maneuvering to offer and give it.
- Leaders exercise creative thinking and creative decision-making.
- Leaders establish Vision, articulate their Message through personal and organizational Mission, and seek to fully cooperate with agreed and shared core Values.
- Leaders believe it can be done.
- Leaders learn from "traditional" thinking, and seek innovation.
- Leaders eagerly accept a challenge and opportunity to do more, and do what they do better.
- Leaders test their views.
- Leaders trust and are trustworthy.
- Leaders understand the essentials of the composite nature of themselves and those they lead, and promote balanced development of the person.
- Leaders are accountable: first to the people they lead before ever requiring accountability from them, and to those in positions of authority over them.
- Leaders believe in and practice loyalty to core values,

relationships, and shared decisions.

- Leaders understand the differences between intangibles, those traits of character that cannot be bought; and tangibles, those material results of product provision (money and what it can purchase) necessary to assure a business's economic success. Leaders realize that intangibles are the motives that give birth to tangible results, that intangibles and tangibles are not in conflict with one another, rather, they are complimentary.
- Leaders associate with other leaders and continually seek advice and counsel of those who have gone before.
- Leaders are mentors and are being mentored.
- Leaders eagerly promote success in others.
- Leaders anticipate problems and proactively create solutions.
- Leaders own solutions and take extra efforts to more than satisfy a customer's or follower's needs.
- Leaders are students who consistently read, ask questions, and listen to answers.
- Leaders act responsibly.
- Leaders are models.
- Leaders willingly submit to authority.
- Leaders purposefully give for the good of those they lead.
- Leaders set realistic expectations of themselves and those they lead.

- Leaders tell the truth.
- Leaders have no need for excessive control; rather, they desire to grow through investment and transfer of ownership.
- Leaders validate principle and obey in practice.
- Leaders speak well of authority over them and those who follow, building up, not tearing down.
- Leaders humble themselves.
- Leaders earn respect, not demand it; grant respect in order to expand it.
- Leaders empower followers to be better and do better.
- Leaders persevere.
- Leaders recognize that their relationship should be their function, and their function their relationship. They strive for complete agreement between the two that actively demonstrates the value of the person first, function second.
- Leaders love.

How much distance exists between what a follower desires in a leader, and what a leader desires in a follower? There is no exclusion here as to status or station; these characteristics above are not and should not be applied just to leaders. These characteristics are to be the same for leaders and followers. Substitute "follower" for leader on all the traits above, and if you are the leader, determine if that kind of follower would be an asset to your group.

Followers look to leaders to learn how to follow before

they look to leaders to learn how to lead. Leaders declare their intent, position themselves as students of principle in submission to values and authority, commit to upholding their standards, then act, earning the right to teach the lessons of the "what," "how," and "why" of leadership, seen first in how they follow. How the leader follows lays the foundation for the follower to aspire to leadership. The leader becomes the teacher because the leader has first been, and remains, a good student. Following well always precedes leading well.

> Followers look to leaders to learn how to follow before they look to leaders to learn how to lead.

Ask a group of people what kind of leader they desire to emulate, and the list usually includes some of these intangible attributes, which many see as values: knowledgeable, wise, caring, open, honest, dedicated, willing to listen, strong, gentle, truthful, available, representative of the group, committed, communicative, flexible, decisive, visionary, able to problem solve, provisionary, exemplary, eager to learn.... What is desired of leaders is to be cultivated into followers, and followers who aspire to leadership adopt the same list for themselves.

Preparing someone else to take his or her place by training committed followers how to grow in solid character traits, follow well and therefore lead well, is the leader's responsibility. Perhaps you will embrace this truth whole-heartedly: Duplication of principle is where values-driven, and therefore valuable, legacy comes into being. A leader for more than a day is never complacent regarding investment into a follower's life; this leader is not content with a mediocre or hands-off approach. Great and long-lasting leadership is seen when a leader's invasion with permission becomes a part of a follower's experience, it can be tracked, and its progress is consistently evaluated within a predetermined time line.

This is What Leadership Is— Introduction
Chapter 1: Who Leaders Are and What Leaders Do—
The Principle of Life-Investment

Review and Reinforce:

1. Investment in the follower is the central nugget of truth in leadership that works and builds legacies that last.
2. Those who are in positions of authority and influence are called upon to responsibly choose the types of people investment in which they will engage themselves and the people they impact.
3. Leadership is a decision.
4. Leadership defined: a state of interaction with others that can and must be cultivated to create duplicative results for positive and regenerating impact.
5. Learning becomes living, and communication is complete when behaviors change.
6. People are more important than what they do, and relationships precede and give definition to function.
7. Relationship is defined as the decision one makes about another's success. Function is the real-life corroboration of the decision.
8. If you were convinced that you were more important than what you do, who would benefit?
9. Great leadership requires a dedication to shared values that far exceeds the tendency to bend to circumstances,

expediency or mere convenience. Ends here do not justify means; in fact, the process here is more important than the product.

10. Leaders believe in investing in people and are ultimate examples of integrity, dedicated to growth in their own selves and those who follow; they exercise accountability, are trustworthy, provide models, are humble, and love.

11. Followers look to leaders to learn how to follow before they look to leaders to learn how to lead.

12. Duplication of principle is where values-driven, and therefore valuable, legacy comes into being.

13. Great and long lasting leadership is seen when a leader's invasion with permission becomes a part of a follower's experience.

2
Leadership Tracks and Traits

Leadership as a place can be seen as attractive and achievable. Leadership as a position can be aspired to and acquired. Leadership as an opportunity to invest into a life is far and away the most admired. It may not be as attractive because it is harder to achieve and more often than not carries significant costs, but when the option is right, it is the most anticipated, appreciated, endearing and enduring form of leadership available.

Leaders pass their batons. It is not an optional activity. The question is not whether the baton is passed; rather, the question is when, how, and to whom, and what the baton represents. Opportunities for creating this engagement outnumber viable options; opportunities must be distilled so that the most workable, those with the greatest potential for success, become the options from which best choices are made. A leader and follower work together in designing the baton and how it will be handed on. This process is intentional, clearly understood, and never assumed.

Because a leader builds legacy to inspire future generations, planning and preparation are imperative. Time is set aside to consider investment and potential for return. Leadership is intentional, so its choices of application are pre-thought, declared openly, and acted upon with dedication. Actions are open to inspection and require accountability. A leader takes initiative to assure that expenditures of time, assets, and effort are invested wisely. A follower knows the leader's intent because the leader has accurately articulated it, and they willfully agree.

Consider three leadership running tracks called Impact, Influence and Investment. Each track represents a place of leadership, and each has its own traits and requirements for leaders and followers.

A runner may cross from track to track at any time, and a leader often exists in more than one leadership-follower relationship track at the same time to accommodate multiple followers' needs and group interactions. The lines between the tracks are merely indications of environment, not inhibitors of engagement. A leader's choice of the tracks in which to run is part of that leader's exercise of judgment, and a wise leader knows what track on which he is running in light of the followers who are being affected at that moment and for the future.

A leader chooses to expend his or her energy on a track based on consideration of the people and product outcome expectation, the quality of the reward at the finish, and the time line needed to accomplish the impact, influence or investment goals. Regardless of the track chosen, and because a baton is always passed, the importance of the quality of relational and functional leadership involved in the choice of tracks cannot be underestimated.

Impact leadership, influence leadership and investment leadership tracks each possess seven categories of delineation, consisting of *Environment, Recognizing the Leader, Leadership Strategy, Relationships with Followers, Function Demonstrating Relationship, Behaviors, and Expectations.* You are invited to join this run, and choose your leadership tracks.

Impact Leadership

Environment: Observation

Recognizing the Leader: Presence

Leadership Strategy: Example

Relationships with Followers: Dependence

Function Demonstrating Relationship: Activities

Behaviors: Seeing Patterns and Classifying Characteristics

Expectation: Maintenance

- Leadership's effects often begin at this point of contact, frequently within a larger-group environment.
- This track is a place where the leader's initial image becomes known and begins its development.

- Followers learn this leader's methods of following and leading through observance.
- A group structure helps define frameworks of activity for the follower and the impact leader.
- The culture of a room is changed when this leader just shows up. The leader's very presence on a team makes a difference, and this impact is often driven by personality and casual contact, as well as observable example.
- Deliverables and their effectiveness are seen more readily in activities focused on production, and prized higher than intricacies and depths of relationships, but this leader considers relationships at deeper levels as networking with groups and individuals progresses.
- Tangibles in product provision are weighted more heavily than intangibles of "seeing the bigger picture," but this leader is awake to intangibles and begins to encourage followers to consider them.
- Here a leader grows toward influence, and at this impact stage core values are first tried and tested as they become recognized as needful, motives are born and nourished, and essential activities provide proof of validity of character.
- There is no time limit on impact leadership, it simply occurs when the leader is in attendance and contributes to the group by example.
- Titles have little significance, if used at all.
- Team or group members will gravitate toward this

leader, and relationships characterized by dependence upon the leader are seen. When the leader moves, the followers move.

- The leader is admired; followers and supervisors size up potential in this leader; alliances are formed.
- The inner-workings of the group's activities give rise to the need for policies and procedures.
- Patterns of individual behaviors are seen and classified according to socially required characteristics of what is acceptable; the leader honors and builds upon these standards.
- Expanded outcomes yield felt needs for goal-driven recognition, and tangible evidences of success are prized (money, gifts, awards and certificates).
- Maintenance of alliances and established patterns of activity become expected within the group.
- The leader whose impact has helped a team achieve production goals is elevated in importance and seen to be one to which others naturally look for stimulus.
- This leader may be pushed toward higher stations, and promotion opportunities loom in this leader's future if these are desired.
- Jealousy emerges as part of the group dynamic as this leader makes a mark; this leader learns how to manage competition and begins to set goals of achievement that eventually, most often in the short term, have the potential to create new and defined positions of authority, and often do.

- Leadership on the impact track contributes to stronger group camaraderie and serves as an entry point for leaders to grow in leadership skills and for followers looking to learn leadership's dynamics. The more dependence is evidenced, the more it is or can be encouraged. It can be overdone, and a developing leader will seek balanced levels of dependence and autonomy.
- The majority of people within a group where impact leadership is taking place may prefer to pace or permanently reside within this track. The risks of engagement are lower, and staying here appears more comfortable. Benefits outweigh costs, results are usually predictable, and for the most part, positive.

Influence Leadership

Environment: Obligation

Recognizing the Leader: Position

Leadership Strategy: Experience and Education

Relationships with Followers: Independence

Function Demonstrating Relationship: Assignments and Assessment

Behaviors: Setting Policies for Control and Compliance

Expectation: Maturity

- Leadership's effects are strengthened in a smaller group environment, and often include technical and/or managerial training and supervision.
- The leader's position is defined on this track, often within a specified organizational structure.
- Followers learn the leader's methods of following and leading through obligatory or willing obedience, grow in exercising autonomy of thought and action within an established framework of expectation, and reach out for levels of independence.
- Even though desiring and, in some cases, declaring independence, followers still want structures that help define their limits and opportunities for the follower and the leader. Organizational tension follows. Degrees and limits of freedom are challenged.
- The leader's authoritative position on a team or in a group is determined by experience, education, command of responsibility, and the capacity to make decisions and follow through.
- Networking inter-group and cross-departmental relations develop at production levels based on working together to complete assigned tasks. The leader looks for opportunities to grow relationships to deeper levels as the leader gets to know those under his or her influence better.
- Intangibles and tangibles mix: intangibles become the articulated "reasons why" a group does what it does as Vision gives birth to Mission; people are busy earning

tangibles while experiencing increasing intangibles of relational depth.

- Here a leader assesses his or her influence, and a job well done points toward additional responsibility and growing people from the inside out.
- There may be a time limit on influence leadership.
- Titles are employed.
- Accountability is higher, and team members know where the buck stops.
- The leader is obeyed through obligation or desire or both. If not, the leader may use position and authority to alter organizational placements.
- The leader's place is decision-sensitive; through the leader's decisions, a framework is designed in which a leader's strength is realized and respect grows as good decisions yield superior results.
- Structures and charts defining authoritative liability, communication paths, and right and wrong actions are set in place; behavioral standards are defined and maintained with policies and procedures to standardize control and compliance.
- The leader scans the team and the performance of its members for true chances to give recognition and appropriate praise.
- Maturing leader and followers grow in their respective understandings of positional relationships and the corresponding opportunities that exist within them for development of knowledge and wisdom.

- The leader's accomplishments are responsibility-driven; the balanced growth of relationships and functional accountability is on the rise, and with success, comes the chance of putting this leader on a pedestal.
- This leader is offered opportunities for expansion of current groups or the creation of new ones.
- Team members follow but may not fully honor the leader's title, position and responsibility; this leader learns how to manage criticism, and while he or she must be interested in discovery of fault and appropriate ownership of consequence on the part of all individuals within the group, the leader concentrates more on solution provision and building relationships.

Investment Leadership
Environment: Opportunity
Recognizing the Leader: Person
Leadership Strategy: Expansion
Relationships with Followers: Inter-Dependence
Function Demonstrating Relationship: Apprenticeship
Behaviors: Sharing Perspectives for Life-Change
Expectation: Modeling

- Leadership's principles and practices are taught to a highly selective few where mentoring and model making are the goals, and personal development is the focus. No more than one to three people can receive investment leadership from any one leader at one time; this leader is learning how to balance relationships and functions and carefully chooses the people into whom investments can occur.

- This track is a place where the leader's position is not nearly as important as his person, and the leader's contributions come from the leader's desire to personally invest; relationships (decisions about supporting others' successes) are other-people-embracing and core values-driven.

- Followers become apprentices, learn the leader's methods of following and leading through willfully engaging in opportunities for growth the leader and followers cooperatively create and are eager to carry out ownership of principle within their own life practices.

- Followers request structures that frame opportunities for the follower and the leader, and the leader takes the initiative to start processes of defining where transfer of ownership occurs.

- The leader's contributions into those selected for investment are model-driven; this leader rejects tendencies toward being placed on a pedestal or building legacies seen only in a monument devoid of living manifestation.

- Relationships develop through a leader and follower's mutual commitments to the process of inter-dependence where the leader looks for ways to give him or herself away to help the follower succeed, assisting the follower to become even more effective than the leader; cooperation along this path replaces any predisposition toward competition that excludes another from reaching a win or defining success by position or place.

- Intangibles come before tangibles in importance and motive. Tangibles become products, not goals. Intangibles thread through every action, seen in heightened levels of trust, affirmation, objective evaluation, and celebration.

- Here a leader consistently evaluates his or her investment with an apprentice; seeing a follower duplicate the model of principle and practice within the follower's own development of method is an inestimable reward. Leadership in this track doesn't care that anyone notices who should or could get the credit or blame; leader and follower silently take up custody of either.

- There is always a time limit on investment leadership. The purpose, goal and mile markers of success are predetermined, and mutually agreed by the participants.

- Titles don't matter.

- Accountability is highest; either or both follower and leader initiate accountability without persuasion or coercion; coaching replaces coaxing, desire replaces demand, opportunity replaces obligation.

- The leader is respected but not worshipped.

- The leader's place is mentoring-sensitive; through the leader's model, a framework is set for replication, and in this track that process commences, is cared for, and comes to completion.
- The leader gives recognition, appropriate praise, and eagerly seeks opportunities to do so.
- The leader's accomplishments are responsibility-driven, seen in conflict resolution based on core values, communication effectiveness based on a desire to close the loop, and attention to detail where people are honored and functions corroborate declared commitments.
- This leader is approached by potential candidates who want to learn what people investment is because they appreciate the model the leader has shown.
- Followers honor this leader; this leader learns how to manage ego, exercise self-control, and receives more genuine satisfaction from seeing a follower succeed than from his or her own achievements.

Leadership Tracks and Traits Chart

Leadership Tracks and Traits:	*Impact*	*Influence*	*Investment*
Environment:	Observation	Obligation	Opportunity
Recognizing the Leader:	Presence	Position	Person
Leadership Strategy:	Example	Experience and Education	Expansion
Relationships with Followers:	Dependence	Independence	Inter-Dependence
Function Demonstrating Relationships:	Activities	Action and Assessment	Apprenticeship
Behaviors:	Seeing Patterns and Classifying Characteristics	Setting Policies for Control and Compliance	Sharing Perspectives for Life-Change
Expectation:	Maintenance	Maturity	Modeling

Three Leadership Tracks and Traits Diagram

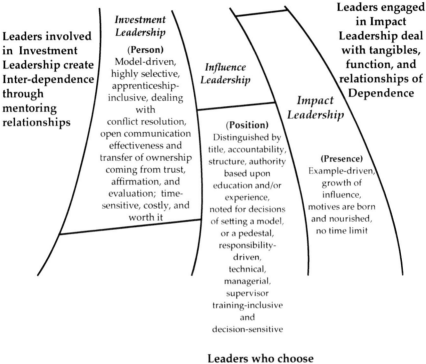

Leaders involved in Investment Leadership create Inter-dependence through mentoring relationships

Investment Leadership

(Person)
Model-driven, highly selective, apprenticeship-inclusive, dealing with conflict resolution, open communication effectiveness and transfer of ownership coming from trust, affirmation, and evaluation; time-sensitive, costly, and worth it

Influence Leadership

Leaders engaged in Impact Leadership deal with tangibles, function, and relationships of Dependence

Impact Leadership

(Position)
Distinguished by title, accountability, structure, authority based upon education and/or experience, noted for decisions of setting a model, or a pedestal, responsibility-driven, technical, managerial, supervisor training-inclusive and decision-sensitive

(Presence)
Example-driven, growth of influence, motives are born and nourished, no time limit

Leaders who choose Influence Leadership deal with Independence, policies and procedures, and growing aspiring leaders

Leaders who want to lead well are individuals who may be engaged with many people at the same time within the impact, influence, and investment leadership tracks, while purposefully looking for the right investment persons and opportunities from within much smaller and selective representations of candidates. The two tracks of impact and influence should be seen as places of quality and arenas of potential. A leader's impact may affect thousands; his or her influence may well inspire many groups, but his or her investments could forever change two or three lives for immense new impact, influence and eventual investment. The investment leadership track is where you, if you are the leader who desires to build legacy, work to move a select few who share your passion along a track wholly dedicated to collective maturity and regeneration of values.

A growing leader has to confront the temptation to try to invest in too many people at one time, with the truth of what really can be accomplished in the investment leadership track. The energy level needed to fulfill an investment engagement in only a single person who makes the grade and then exceeds expectations is enormous, but worth it.

Because one of the hallmarks of an investment leader is balance of relationship and function, the leader for more than a day knows that the means of carefully seeking and identifying the right person, place, time, motive, method and reward are not optional activities, they are essential to success and must be weighed and incorporated if investment is even to be considered.

Great leaders conduct careful appraisals to know whether or not to encourage movement for a follower from a track of receiving impact or influence into a track of investment, and to weigh the commitment such a movement requires from both leader and follower. Clearly not all followers are candidates for this kind of growth—but some assuredly are, and those who show this potential are the ones where seeds for leadership duplication should be planted.

Leadership that builds lasting legacies is accomplished through people who want to grow. Knowing which of the followers to even ask the questions as to potential for movement is a challenge for every leader who desires to build legacies that last. Enduring leadership seeks investment potential people. While leaders want to be available and extend help within reasonable extent to those who may not wish for more progression than living within impact and influence, the leader with vision has a primary focus firmly and formally placed on those that earnestly desire more maturity, and show the leader that they long for it.

If you are the leader, consider: What are the tracks on which you are running most of the time, and who is running with you in each track? What evidences have those who follow you shown of their desires to expand their horizons and develop in maturity to become living legacies?

This is What Leadership Is—
Chapter 2: Leadership Tracks and Traits

Review and Reinforce:

1. Leadership is an opportunity to invest.
2. Leadership is intentional.
3. The question is not whether the baton is passed; rather, the question is when, how, and to whom, and what the baton represents.
4. Because a leader builds legacy to inspire future generations, planning and preparation are imperative.
5. In consideration of three leadership tracks, a leader chooses to expend his or her energy on a track based on consideration of the people and product outcome expectation, the quality of the reward at the finish, and the time line needed to accomplish the impact, influence or investment goals.
6. *Impact Leadership:* an environment of observation where a leader is recognized by his or her presence, the strategy is example, where relationships with followers are ones of dependence, and the function demonstrating relationship is activity; the behaviors constitute seeing patterns and classifying their characteristics, and the expectation is maintenance.
7. *Influence Leadership*: an environment of obligation where a leader is recognized by position, the strategy is experience and education, where relationships with

followers are ones of independence, and the function demonstrating relationship is assignments and their assessment; setting policies and control and compliance regulate behaviors, and the expectation is maturity.

8. *Investment Leadership:* an environment of opportunity where a leader is recognized by his or her person, the strategy is expansion, where relationships with followers are ones of inter-dependence, and the function demonstrating relationship is apprenticeship; sharing perspectives for life change become common behaviors, and modeling is the expectation.

9. A leader's impact may affect thousands, his or her influence may well inspire many groups and his or her investments could forever change two or three lives for the better.

10. Enduring and investment-oriented leadership seeks investment-potential people.

3
Investment Leadership Initiative

Living Proof: "John, Paul and Leadership Initiative"

John was a middle manager in a large contracting firm, in charge of maintenance and new construction on the properties the company managed in six sectors of twenty-four in their region. One of his greatest challenges was managing his time; there was always more to accomplish than time seemed to permit. Field supervisors demanded his on-site coaching and training; his boss possessed ever-abounding energy and micro-managed John's work, constantly "needed to know" the minutiae... bottom line, the boss was a detractor, and may have not even known it, even though he had confidence in John's product.

For John, the pull came from multiple sources, up, across, and down. When meeting with his peers, other region sector managers, they commiserated on their similarities of work environment demands; in fact, a lot of whining and complaining took place. The attitudes they displayed among themselves put tension where trust should have been, and none of them came away from those conversations better for it; in fact, their collective griping negatively impacted those who looked to them for example-setting.

At a management improvement seminar, John was introduced to three tracks of leadership. As he analyzed them, he realized he was running on the impact and influence tracks, but felt he had no time to even consider an engagement on the investment track. Then he thought about Paul, one of his field supervisors, who seemed to be earnest to develop into more of a contributor and personal learner. John wrestled with it, but how does one carve out time for investment leadership when there is no time? And how would other managers perceive his actions?

To even consider investing in any worthy candidate, John knew he had to re-prioritize his attitudes and calendar and work on balancing his energy output, concentrate on setting boundaries to contain or eliminate unnecessary demands fostered on him, and make time for investment if he was serious. This process would not be easy but he decided to proceed, somehow convinced that it was the right move.

First came a meeting with his boss who, because he re-spected John's output, gave him time for discussion. John de-scribed the three leadership tracks and told his boss that Paul appeared to be ready for John to lead him through investment; that to do this, John would reallocate portions of his time in a specific schedule that John would communicate clearly and regularly with his superior. John committed to looking for additional opportunities to "clean up" his calendar by transferring ownership of some of his tasks to his administrative assistance team, explaining what was up. John's boss agreed based on John's conditions and commitments. Implementing the transitions of time allocation took two weeks of careful planning before the preliminary process was completed, but finally the calendar had some room.

When John approached Paul about investment leadership, Paul was more eager than John supposed he would be, and the investment, targeted to last three months and then subject to review and reconstitution if successful, began.

Accountability for John in planning his procedure had become first priority before seriously thinking about entering the investment leadership track with Paul. Because he planned well and declared his intent and method to his boss and members of his own team, he had come to Paul with agreements in place that would allow leadership through investment the greatest chance of success. John's self control, adjusting his priorities to serve another, and following well had fostered solid launching points for a model of leadership investment John wanted to create and Paul wanted to receive. Plus, John's actions had set an example to his peers. Focusing on using time better for the benefit of another started to replace a lot of whining.

It all began with the leader.

An investor leader takes the initiative, period. Sometimes the action that this initiative produces may be interpreted as "pushy" or "type-A driven," and well it could be. Regardless, there is no other option for the leader who wants to make a difference through investing in a follower's life; he or she will take initiative and think and act proactively from a solution oriented perspective, or the investment simply will not happen.

Initiative in varying degrees will be required on each leadership track for a leader who participates on any. Initiative increases, however, as leader and followers consider expanded investment options in the investment leadership track. Within this track, initiative as a mark of leadership becomes the most evidenced trait, and sets the pace for growth.

Initiative within investment leadership has its own set of attributes, and in comparison to these a leader's degree of initiative can be measured.

Attributes of Investment Leadership Initiative

Investment Leadership Initiative:

1. Doesn't wait for followers to say they want leadership's contributions, it pursues the followers to see if they do when potential is evident.
2. Is respectful but firm as it addresses issues that seek to thwart progress.

3. Sets realistic time lines for itself and its followers, and expects these to be fulfilled.

4. Tells and accepts the truth; responds to success with gladness and to error with efforts to correct it.

5. Positions a realistic pace by giving followers projects and programs that each require in succession a degree of additional effort, expanded learning and mental stretching.

6. Does not dwell in excuses for inaction, nor allow followers who want to grow to dwell in a holding pattern; rather, promotes experiences of ownership transfer, willingness to take on assignments, earnest desires for learning, eagerness of participation, and possibilities to overcome obstacles.

7. Is committed to verification of expected results in a predetermined time frame.

8. Puts people first proactively.

9. Desires to be on the receiving end of another's investments, seeks wisdom from others who teach, listens intently, learns thoroughly, and applies carefully.

10. Understands the differences between incidents and issues, and moves each important incident (task or occurrence) to its underlying issue (relationship, decision, cause) for purposes of clarification, confrontation, commitment to action, correction, and commendation.

11. Refuses a "one size fits all" formula to acquiring or exercising leadership; while principle driven, it promotes flexibility of application.

12. Defines the framework into which its investments can be created.

The Law of Sowing and Reaping and the Law of Compensation

Investment leadership initiative derives its being from the models within the Law of Sowing and Reaping and the Law of Compensation. Both are natural laws and high principles. The Law of Sowing and Reaping states that whatever leaders invest into the right soil will be multiplied back in a ratio of many to one. The Law of Compensation says that sure and compensatory reward will follow every action.

Each leader, in consideration of the concepts presented here, views leadership as a venture of elevated importance, one that contains lasting effect, and yields return in duplicative fashion and like manner, exponentially. Leadership's investment carefully considers selections of person, time, place and opportunity and these choices are fulfilled within expanding knowledge (understanding what to do), wisdom (knowing how to do it) and care (anticipating and projecting how what is done will affect others), because results will surely follow.

Emerson has stated, "Every act rewards itself... Cause

and effect, means and ends, seed and fruit, cannot be severed; for the effect already blooms in the cause, the end preexists in the means, the fruit in the seed... The nature and soul of things takes on itself the guaranty of the fulfillment of every contract, so that honest service cannot come to loss... Every stroke shall be repaid..."

This model of leadership investment is exclusive and inclusive at the same time. It is exclusive in that it appropriately limits the most transferable investments and greatest vision casting to a narrowed number of followers who have the most opportunity for impact, influence and investment in others with what they have learned; it is inclusive in that the message of core values and people investment, its operational truth-in-action, and the successes of the leader's involvement with the follower are openly presented to a wide audience through the actions of the followers into their networks. People into whom future exclusive investments are made will most likely come out of this wider audience of observers. This cycle of leadership investment becomes a repeating pattern, from leader to follower, and new leader to new follower.

If you are an investor leader, you will own the responsibility to take the initiative to begin a process of life investment into a follower. This process is not casual; rather, it is cause-driven. It is intentional invasion with permission into another person's life and experience.

Within this investment model, three distinct yet related action steps are to be considered and completed for results to become legacy:

- **Qualify** those into and through whom investments will occur.
- **Quality Investments** designed for long lasting effects, must be generated.
- **Quantify** the investment through objective evaluation.

This is What Leadership Is—
Chapter 3:
Investment Leadership Initiative

Review and Reinforce:

1. An investor leader takes the initiative.
2. There is no other option for the leader who wants to make a difference through investing in a follower's life; he or she will take initiative and think and act proactively from a solution-oriented perspective, or the investment simply will not happen.
3. Initiative pursues.
4. Investment Leadership Initiative is balanced between receiving and giving, and desires both.
5. Excuses for inaction are not allowed.
6. Initiative is committed to principle in its foundation and flexibility in its application.
7. Investment Leadership Initiative defines the framework into which its investments can be created.
8. Investment Leadership Initiative derives its being from the models within the Law of Sowing and Reaping and the Law of Compensation.
9. A leader owns the responsibility to take the initiative to begin a process of life investment into a follower.
10. Initiative engages in intentional invasion with permission into another person's life and experience.

4
Qualifying Trials

Those who wish to run in the investment track will go through qualifying trials. These assessments provide up to the moment snapshots that determine potential, starting positions and opportunities for success.

Choosing people who have the most promise for success is one of the first responsibilities of the investment leader. This process requires wisdom, diligence in observation, purposeful questions of candidates, and strong character that is not easily moved and certainly does not sacrifice principled values when circumstances change.

A leader who desires to build legacy obtains permission and willing agreement to invest from the right people into whom to invest. This permission and agreement lead to prospects of deeper learning and eventual transfer of ownership of key concepts into real practice when the follower's learning becomes living.

Five Criteria for Investment Leadership

Five criteria constitute the qualifying trials for a leader and follower who want to run in the investment leadership track together. In this selection-for-mentoring process, a thorough examination within these criteria is strongly recommended. If you are the leader, look for:

1. *People of impact and influence*

   These are people who impact others by their presence, sometimes whether or not they desire to do so. Certainly those who command attention and are articulate, whom people admire, and who may have positional influence over and with others because of who they are and what they do, are candidates.

2. *People who possess a track record of growing maturity and faithfulness*

   Their lives are exemplary in that they show diligence toward living according to shared core values, are moving toward maturity out of a sincere desire for personal development, possess a growing understanding of what it means to be faithful, and regard their responsibilities to model faithfulness with unwavering commitment.

3. *People who are shown to be stable and accountable*

   Stability and accountability are attributes of rising relational and functional maturity. Stability is shown when the relational decisions toward being a person of trust and truth are given context and illustration in outward demonstration in dealings with others. Accountability is stability in duplicative action: it is ongoing and able to be repeated. Real life accountability in a recurring pattern of faithfulness is the evidence of personal core stability. Stability is shown in accountability through consistent truth telling, actions that demonstrate words, reliability, following through by accomplishing details, loyalty, and devotion.

4. *People who are humble and teachable*

Humility is an individual's choice. People who are becoming disciplined to humble themselves realize they need to learn and are, therefore, teachable. They understand that what they don't know exceeds what they do know, and are eager to position themselves as students. Only humble students grow to become investor-teachers. Humility is one of those traits that can't trumpet its own existence. You should never hear, "Read my book on humility and how I attained it." If a person is humble, that person knows, and that person's network knows, it is rarely discussed, although it is often affirmed.

5. *People whose life-season is appropriate to being able to receive and give leadership investment*

There are seasons when investments are appropriate and, conversely, times when they are not. Wise leadership looks to understand the life-seasons of the followers under consideration for leadership and leadership training, openly and honestly discusses whether their season is right for both the receiving of leadership truths and deliverables, and the dissemination of these truths into the lives and work experiences of others. Leaders for more than today seek and apply wisdom to discover the timing and season for the right person, place, time, motive, method and reward.

An investor-leader looks not for perfection, but for balance in an individual who desires growth, and applies these qualifiers to him or herself first. Demonstrated perseverance is the key. If any of the above five criteria are not present in a follower, or absent in a leader, then history, desire or potential that is not there should not be falsely manufactured. Blatant shortcomings in any of the above say that chances are high that negative consequences and fruitless expended energy could well be the result over time. Waste not.

Living Proof: "Jeanette and the Administrative Support Group"

Jeanette had been a part of the Administrative Support Group (ASG) for three years. The support group's thirty-five members were tasked with supplying needed customer service, secretarial, ordering, and bookkeeping support for the sales and marketing division of a large international firm. Explosive growth within the company had strained the resources of the ASG when the group numbered only twenty-two. In a recent six-month time frame, to help create enhanced administrative production, thirteen new hires had been retained, and after each had passed their ninety-day probation period, were on line and functioning.

At this time, the ASG consisted essentially of a collection of two populations of individuals, one "old" that had been with the company for three years or more, and one "new" that had been with the company six months or less. The ASG had been moving to streamline operations, and the general attitude was one of anticipation and acceptance of new technology, trying to work smarter not harder, and employing greater customer service deliverables to the international sales and marketing division, scattered in seven regions world-wide.

Jeanette was a member of the "old" group, and had been assigned training duties for the new hires through their periods of probation. In her trainer role, she was at first uncomfortable because she was one who enjoyed working alone, preferring completing tasks herself "to make sure they got done right." Now it became one of her jobs to help other people succeed. In that respect, she became a leader, but at first a non-enthusiastic one. Regardless, she trained and they learned. It was a good experience, and people noticed.

It was one thing for Jeanette to train new workers to master technical requirements of their new positions. It was another entirely when Jeanette's boss came to her with a directive to consolidate resources, and incorporate "new" and "old" people into seven ASG Teams, each team to serve one region of sales and marketing personnel, while interfacing with one another to assure timely response and provide accurate checks and balances. Matching skill sets, personality cooperativeness and needed space to create teams that would work well seemed, at first, to be overwhelming considerations to this new leader who had been content to just get work done in isolation. Growth of the company, however, demanded change, and created expansion opportunities for Jeanette on a relational as well as functional basis, even though she didn't yet completely understand that idea.

While Jeanette knew she had experienced good success with the technical training of the new hires, she felt that at this stage she did not enjoy the full confidence of the entire ASG, primarily because her former isolation had been fairly effective until pushed training needs forced a new environment upon her. With this new team directive, she concluded she had to earn respect from the wider group, and sought a way to accomplish this goal.

The efforts she put forth to earn the esteem of two diverse and divided working cultures were exemplary. They began with Jeanette designing a survey in combination with confidential one-on-one interviews for every employee in the ASG. She wanted to know the quality of relational strengths within her organization, which the survey addressed, and the excellence of functional achievement, analyzed in the results of the information acquired through the interviews. Making this composite image was time-consuming, but she felt her results would prove worth the effort.

During this time, she attended a seminar where the idea of three tracks of leadership was presented, and determined to apply the definitions of impact leadership, influence leadership, and investment leadership with herself and her entire group, in hopes of finding investment opportunities. Jeanette told the entire ASG about the tracks, and that she would be using these in the process of fulfilling her new assignment.

As the interviews began, she purposefully started to look for seven leaders out of a pool of thirty-five into whom she could commit extended training, so that these seven would then contribute to their respective groups and build on the success of Jeanette's investment in them. Her interviews and surveys had started her on a new path of people engagement, and she grew excited about where this venture could lead.

Jeanette had decided to become a leader of leaders.

As she interviewed each employee, she expressed genuine interest in what they had to say; she listened intently, she was engaged in their explanations of celebrations, as well as their concerns. In the course of the interviews, she began to learn who wished to excel, she evaluated potential on the basis of whether the candidates were shown to be people of impact and influence, whether they were growing in their maturity and faithfulness, were stable with prominent accountability, and at the same time showed humility, were teachable, and appeared and declared that they were ready to embark on a track of investment leadership development.

She carefully weighed how best to position these thirty-five people into quality teams so that all seven sales and marketing regions would be served from combined strengths. Analysis of the data was accomplished, and at its conclusion, Jeanette determined that eight people qualified for investment leadership. She set a program and time line in place to run in the investment track with these new leaders, and obtained each person's agreement to proceed.

Seven groups and eight new leaders—this was more success than she had anticipated. Cross training and duplication produced a rotation of alternates, where one was "in the wings" at all times. A dearth of leaders was transformed into a depth of new leadership experience, and the beginnings of a legacy.

To accomplish this venture of discovery, it had taken committed effort, energy, extra time and genuine interest in the success of these eight additional leaders to create a structure where they would apply new tools, grow through the process, and provide leadership depth. Jeanette's success was not only seen in the redesigned organizational configuration she implemented, but also in her attitudes toward her peers and those accountable to her; her former reclusive nature had been converted into new inclusive nurture as she replaced isolation with inclusion.

Communication with directors and staff in each of the seven regions grew to new heights; order processing, customer service, product delivery and accounting were tracked with greater accuracy; and mistakes, while not eliminated, became an exception. The ASG saw itself as seven teams designed to pave pathways of ongoing success for the entire firm. This could never have happened if Jeanette had not changed her own perspective from exclusion centered on what she desired for herself to what was good for others who wanted to grow from her strength, who would benefit the whole organization.

Leadership attaches great importance to investment where resilient growth is desired and a willingness to stretch is present.

It is far better for you, the leader, to participate in forthright and up-front discussions about real possibilities and the enormous responsibilities of an investment endeavor than it is to attempt to create return within a person who does not have the purpose or passion for more. It is reassuring that a person who does desire growth but who may not be ready yet for this degree of investment can embark on a journey of becoming qualified, and a leader will encourage this decision, and support its progress.

The investment leadership track requires full agreement and dedication from the leader and the follower once a decision has been made to start the run. Once a leader and follower have passed the qualification trials, the leader moves to initiate the action of the investment within the investment leadership track. It is hard work for both; building legacies is not easy, but carries remarkable rewards.

This is What Leadership Is—
Chapter 4:
Qualifying Trials

Review and Reinforce:

1. A great leader obtains permission and willing agreement from the right people into whom to invest.
2. Leaders look for people of impact and influence.
3. Leaders look for people who possess a track record of growing maturity and faithfulness.
4. Leaders look for people who are shown to be stable and accountable.
5. Leaders look for people who are humble and teachable.
6. Leaders look for people whose life-season is appropriate to being able to receive and give leadership investment.
7. An investor-leader looks not for perfection, but for balance in an individual who desires growth, and applies these qualifiers to him or herself first.
8. The investment run will require total understanding, agreement, and dedication from both parties.

5
Quality Investments

Generating quality investments is a rewarding and multifaceted task for the investment leader. Quality Investments are part of the constitution of investment leadership and include knowledge, understanding, and application of the Code of Achievement: the "whys, whats, and hows" of accomplishing a worthwhile project, properly establishing authority and accountability, relational investment into the lives of learners, functional responsibility, open lines of communication, cooperative problem solving and conflict resolution, and creating realistic expectations of results.

The Code of Achievement

The Code of Achievement is a compilation of the elements needed to build a legacy: values, vision, mission, and message. To produce quality investments, a leader and follower possess a clear understanding of the definition and inter-workings of these four vital fundamentals. In the investment leadership track the Code of Achievement makes up the character of the baton that the leader passes to the follower.

1. *Values* constitute the core principles upon which agreement exists between leader and follower and are made up of intangibles that never change.
2. *Vision* describes an overall purpose, the reasons why actions are considered, and the hopes for what the future can be in goal accomplishment. Through vision, cause and motive give meaning to activity.
3. *Mission* is made up of the tasks to complete, the methods used to achieve their goals, the evaluations that show success or failure, and the tangible rewards to be received when the mission is accomplished.
4. *Message* represents life-lessons learned through the fulfillment of the mission that impact people with truth. Message is the acquired knowledge that is applied with wisdom.

Leadership implanted into the lives of followers who are eager and positioned well to receive the investment builds upon unfailing comprehension, agreement and application of all four elements of the code of achievement simultaneously. Efforts to keep these four in focus take time, enterprise and determination. A great leader exercises initiative and reinforcement of the code of achievement because that leader is certain that investments based on values, vision, mission, and message work, even though results may not be, and often are not, seen immediately.

Motivation results when all four essentials of the code of achievement are engaged together on the investment leadership track. This motivation empowers a disciplined follower toward ownership of the purpose and procedures with the leader, and develops both shared responsibility and reward. Bottom line: When the code of achievement is implemented fully, the baton is passed.

Integration of all four elements is not optional if an investment is to yield the highest return. A legacy is formed when the baton is passed with integrity and the assurance that it will be held and its meaning upheld. A leader for more than a moment takes the initiative to consistently integrate all four elements into an investment run because the experience and the future demand it.

Values become the grid against which all activities are measured to determine inherent or acquired worth. *Vision* is articulated by the leader at all stages of investment to keep the "reasons why" in frontal perspective. Wisdom literature states, "Where there is no vision, the people perish…" (Proverbs 29:18a; *Holy Bible*: KJV). An alternate version of this sentence reads: "Where there is no revelation, the people cast off restraint…" (NIV). Seeing what is ahead, and why the intention to completing the process matters, initiates disciplined dedication to accomplish the **mission** and receive the reward for doing so. Actions to fulfill the mission that originate from the unerring cooperation of values and vision, demonstrate concert of thought and deed. Throughout the process, a **message** of truth emerges, life lessons are disseminated. When these elements become living truths, the code of achievement has been instilled and fulfilled, the baton has been passed and the process is ready to be instigated again from within a leader who began as a follower, and has learned how to lead. The legacy is established.

Properly Establishing Authority and Accountability

The course of properly establishing authority creates and clarifies lines of relational accountability and functional supervisory management with those positioned above the leader, across from the leader (peers), and those with positions designated under the leader. If you are the leader, you are relationally accountable to all of these and functionally accountable to most, if not all, of them.

Creating strong accountability structures is critical to building foundations of responsibility and respect where decisions are given freedom of expression, and where responsibility for success or failure can be willfully owned. When responsibility is honored, authority and accountability are never separated.

A leader's job is to define clear lines of authoritative

and accountability structures. These lines are necessary for modeling investment, submission and obedience to occur.

Structures for leader and follower must be sensitive to talents and gifting, the essentials of an individual's composite nature (experience, education, and environment), personality and communication methods, job descriptions, realistic expectations, and quantified results. Correctly designed authoritative and accountability structures provide maximum opportunities for investment and encouragement in the pursuit of excellence.

Authority and Accountability Chart

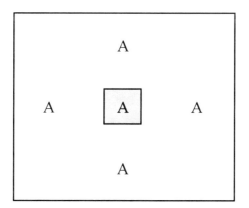

1. If you are the leader, you are always in the middle position as a person who is accountable to authority, as well as a person who possesses authority, and the responsibility that accompanies the position. In this structure, it is easy to see how followers look to leaders

to learn how to follow before followers look to leaders to learn how to lead.

2. The A on the top represents the person or entity to which you are accountable and who has authority over you. Every leader has a person or group to which he or she is accountable. If a leader does not have this structure, that leader doesn't know how to follow and should not be instructing followers.

3. The A on either side represents your peers, those with whom you share responsibility. These people look to you, the leader, to build confidence, and are often the ones who see what really makes you tick. Authenticity is most readily seen among your peers.

4. The A on the bottom denotes the person or group over which you exercise authority. The follower who wants to be the leader's apprentice often comes from this position. It is this person to whom you take the initiative to be accountable before requiring accountability from him or her. Leadership accountability to the people it leads earns the right to be heard and followed.

Lines and positions of authority and accountability are not to be seen as limiting, rather, unlocking as to growth of responsibility and open communication. Investment leadership upholds atmospheres that encourage over environments that squelch. Where a leader is confident enough to share, the leader molds and supports opportunities for success in his or her followers and helps to create atmospheres that promote, if not prod, advancement. Where leaders are insecure and feel threatened, especially where progress of followers is perceived as perilous to a leader's position, work settings are fashioned that stifle growth, impede communication, and smother opportunity for maturity as a leader's lack of courage hides the cause.

A leader for more than the expedient becomes deliberately and seriously involved in building organizational structures to empower investor-leaders and followers who aspire to learning. Positions and titles, while sometimes necessary, are not as important as recognition that for a defined period of time a leader is conducting actions designed to make the follower better, and qualify the follower to own the baton when the time comes.

A follower within this kind of reinforcing structure is free to become a responsible, faithful, dedicated and committed learner. This framework, to use an illustration from the art world, provides the space on a canvas where teacher and student, leader and follower, can paint the picture they truly desire, which the frame is destined to enhance, not cover.

Relational Investment into the Lives of Learners

Relational strength is defined by the quality of the decision a leader makes for the benefit of the life and experience of the follower who wants to mature. When the follower agrees with this definition the door is opened to investment.

Relational investment begins with mutual agreement on this definition of success. Encouragement in this context is more than mere words; it is intentionally becoming involved in the life of another with his or her permission to observe, teach, correct, and mentor that person. The leader seeks to become the model to the follower of what both the follower and leader agree is that to which the follower should aspire. Encouragement, therefore, consists of the leader's decision to give him or herself away, and the active follow-through to become accountable to the individual into whom the leader is investing.

Relational investment begins by asking and obtaining answers to four critical questions from an investment candidate. Not intended to corner or serve as threats, these questions are designed to open discussions as to potential for growth and serve as assessment tools to learn the degrees of opportunity for success.

Whenever these questions are employed with integrity the stage is set for healthy discussion. Using them is strongly encouraged.

The Four Questions

1. **Who are you at your core?**

   This is a question of **values.** This question seeks to know the heart-core of the individuals, what makes them tick, what are their principled, unchangeable, bedrock beliefs upon which their entire world-view and actions are based. In a trustworthy candidate, these values will likely include but not be limited to intangibles of integrity, trust, commitment, faithfulness, respect, cooperation and love.

2. **What are you called to accomplish?**

This is a question of **vision**. Vision gives purpose. Where this question is answered with a list of tangibles, the candidate is veering off course. Accomplishments are heart-related when they seek to build up other people and accomplish goals through investment. Vision is best described in intangibles. If a candidate refers to benefits seen in values as opposed to benefits seen in valuables, the question and answer are hitting home.

3. **What do you want?**

This is a question of **mission**. Missions are actions to fulfill a goal, and their accomplishment is seen in their effects, both materially and within a frame of mind. What a follower wants should be in direct correlation to the answers to the first two questions. The mission will include hard work and the satisfaction coming from completing a job well. Happiness should be evidenced in tangible rewards—the products of achievement—along with intangible inner repose—an assurance of attainment, a healthy sense of pride in the fulfillment of purpose.

4. Whom will you impact?

This is a question of **message**. Lessons learned are worth little until they become operative in real life. People long for and appreciate authenticity when actions verify words. People who are impacted for good because of a follower's or leader's life model can find themselves in a state of receptivity for learning what, how, and why something or someone worked. Principled truth that invades and transforms life makes people take notice, and for those who desire more than mediocrity, creates hunger for more of whatever "that" is and wherever "it" came from. Message is seen through measures and methods. Message is enfolded into desires, decisions and deeds. The life-lessons learned and taught to those who observe and want to receive them, become the message.

If your goal as an investor-leader is to build upon a foundation that lasts beyond circumstance and creates legacies that matter, then your discussion surrounding the four questions and their answers takes on preliminary and primary importance for you and the one to receive from you. You will ask that the candidate understands and intertwines the Code of Achievement and the Four Questions as he or she considers a leadership experience from a holistic point of view. Upon embarking on the run, you become the empowering agent and a wholly supportive encourager.

None of the four questions can be answered "yes" or "no" and this is a positive attribute of their construction and contribution. These open-ended questions are fashioned to strengthen individual ownership of responsibility and create an environment for self-starting and victory that disallows, and in fact, obliterates propensity toward entitlement or victimization.

Victimization and Victory

There are rock-solid differences between victimization and victory. All achievers experience some degrees of difficulty that challenge character and make life hard at the time. Problem points can include severe pain, disappointment, loss of treasure or treasured relationships, can shake confidence, instill fear and foreboding, and in the extreme threaten one's very existence. Overcoming these problem-source events or circumstances may not be easy, often is not, and perhaps the process is never fair.

Conquering victimization is not the denial that real problems existed or are extant. Choosing victimization is the decision to live within a state where an individual stays within walls of insecurity the problems cause, and uses these walls as excuses to not mature through the problem by confronting it. Victims enjoy company and seek to bring people down to their level of misery, focusing primarily on pain as opposed to potential.

Victory is a state of being where chosen character rises above circumstance and history, learns from the past, and presses forward. People of victory are people who persevere. The state of victory is not composed primarily of a feeling of euphoria brought about by situations that change, but by changes within people. Victory is best seen when an individual embraces and confronts a problem or challenge head on.

Growth and maturity become evident through processes that may include forgiveness, willful behavior alteration, fighting for principle, problem resolution, restitution of relationships, or any combination of these. An individual who becomes better as a result of having lived the lessons and made the choices to embrace the experiences, endure through them and learn from them is living in victory, regardless of circumstances.

The four questions help a follower and leader know where an investment candidate "lives" in the sense of well-being, readiness, eagerness, and fundamental worth. The four questions help determine whether or not this person is living within the right place and time for investment and possesses the proper motives to engage the best methods for achievement.

If a potential investment candidate lives in victimization, the four questions, if answered with integrity, will help point this out. It is better to know *before* you decide to go onto the investment track. Victims must choose victory to be in the best position to receive investment leadership and the process of implementing that choice can be extremely difficult, require dedicated help, take maximum efforts, and a great amount of time. Leaders who see beyond the moment of difficulty encourage those who believe they are victims to begin a victory process and obtain the assistance they need to start to live in hope and assurance. That help may indeed come from the leader or one the leader endorses.

Those who have chosen victory and who want to grow are in a great place to meet and exceed the agreed expectations of an investment paradigm. They will greet this opportunity with enthusiasm and energy. A leader building legacy works with people when they are ready.

Relational investment into qualified candidates takes time, talent, treasure, and is ultimately defined in acts of giving to a follower who desires to receive with gratitude and grace. Relational investment is costly and when done right, so worth it.

Nurture and Support

A process of relational investment will encompass acts of nurture and support, especially in times of difficulty or heightened challenge. Chance dealings are not where these acts occur; they are decidedly intentional and willfully accepted intrusions. In their commitments to the success of the investment, the leader and follower commit to providing both when they are needed.

Nurture is help offered from the outside in and consists of invasive engagement into real life situations, where because objective observation has shown that help is needed, help is offered and accepted. Nurture can be perceived as painful or uncomfortable, as it is to a plant that needs to be pruned or sprayed.

Support is assistance initiated from the inside out, where a leader sees the follower's need because he or she knows the follower well, has identified with the follower's predicament, recognizes solution potential, and lifts a follower to heights of understanding through encouragement and coaching, promoting new accomplishments in spite of negative circumstances. The leader supports the follower because the leader and follower have agreed to grow together on this investment of inter-dependence, and nothing will be allowed to stand in the way of that support becoming reality.

So much of the success of relational investment depends on inter-dependence and the agreements that exist between the leader and follower. This inter-dependence begins when the leader requests and obtains permission from the follower to enter and pursue the follower's quest for leadership. Permission granted, and agreement obtained, are not optional steps. When permission is present, trust and truth-telling develop within an atmosphere of genuine, success-dedicated, and caring accountability.

Investment success comes from conscious decisions to make mutual commitments about the efforts to reach the goal. The follower willingly becomes engaged in submission and humility as part of granting permission for the leader to input his or her life, and the leader assumes the responsibility of taking the follower under his or her wing to teach and train what the leader knows.

A Checklist of Actions for Relational Investment Success

If there were a checklist that could assure success of a relational investment, these ten actions would be presented as needful:

1. Establishing and agreeing on the goal of the investment
2. Communicating this goal in a language both leader and follower understand
3. Authentically demonstrating that the follower's success is more important than the leader's action
4. Actively seeking the right time to invest
5. Responding to felt need, while seeking to understand real need, and allowing the processes of discovery to grow slowly if necessary
6. Asking and answering open-ended questions with integrity
7. Listening intently
8. Thinking with solution mind-sets and using words that

promote success in the creation of mutually agreeable, realistic expectations

9. Creating availability and gentle invasion points throughout the process

10. Encouraging, appreciating and celebrating successes, regardless of size, whenever they occur

Functional Responsibility

Functional Responsibility is a direct result of correct relational investment and becomes evident as truth principle comes alive in real deeds. Actions speak what words declare, and authenticity is seen as transferable models are built. A leader who is building legacy will embody functional responsibility before ever requiring it, and sets the standard for measuring accountability by serving the follower.

A leader recognizes that his or her model will not be perfect, remembering that perfection is not the goal. A leader will err. And when a leader makes mistakes, the leader owns them. Part of owning: apologizing (owning the accountability for an error), seeking forgiveness, receiving it, and moving on.

Functional responsibility includes understanding the respective parts all parties play in correcting error; none are in isolation. An atmosphere of functional responsibility represents a best-opportunity phase to own roles of resolution where accountability is desired. Integrity in ownership of error opens the door to designing an environment that welcomes deeper communication so all can learn from the moment and apply that learning to the next.

A leader takes the initiative to correct an error of his or her making. Going through a process of assuming accountability does not show weakness, rather, meekness (strength under control), and provides little room for victimization or excuses.

A leader's strength of accountability is rooted and revealed from deep and honest character. A leader who makes an error and owns its resolution will not possess a wavering image that seeks to shift the blame. Strength in ownership and correction of error is not a matter of style, rather, substance. Functional responsibility requires substance.

There are many processes of human behavior where functional accountability will illustrate how principles endure. When applied, behaviors are altered. Leadership invested well into followers who are learning and growing will produce uplifting expectations of behavioral change from both leader and follower.

Expectations of Behavioral Change

Expectations of behavioral change will likely include:

1. **Restoring right relationships**

    Relationships that are strained and affect a follower's capability to learn or a leader's ability to model must be dealt with appropriately. It is impossible to teach where significant relationships are torn, and to receive where distance is not bridged.

2. **Doing what is promised when it is promised**

    Authenticity of character is most readily observed when words and actions corroborate each other. If they don't, it is incumbent on leader and follower to change behaviors to align attitude, decision and action. Learning becomes life when behaviors cooperate with principle.

3. **Increased discipline in thought and action**

    Heightened personal discipline begins with thoughts and is demonstrated by deeds. There is no distance between these as one gives birth to the other. A maturing person desires discipline in both.

4. **Desires to give for the welfare of others with a view to beginning the same kind of investment in someone about whom the student or follower cares**

    When a follower is receiving from a leader/investor, a natural inclination as the process unfolds is for the follower to want to benefit another follower of his or her own in similar ways. Timing is important, and when the apprentice is ready, the second level training should begin.

5. **Encouragement transferred into the lives of others**

    Encouragement possesses the most validity when the one who seeks to encourage has walked the path of the one who needs the encouragement. An investment leader sympathizes when possible, empathizes all the time, and never uses sympathy or empathy as other than encouragements to pursue excellence and transfer ownership of solutions into the follower who desires maturity.

6. **Speaking truth in an atmosphere of relational care**

   Truth can be spoken in any atmosphere. An investment leader who cares more about the follower than his or her need to speak cold truth in a relational vacuum, speaks needed truth in a manner that demonstrates care for the follower. Gentleness and forbearance are tools a leader chooses when combining truth with compassion.

7. **Developing a pattern of disciplined giving, born of an attitude of thanksgiving**

   Gratitude for an investment is seen in words of thanks and works of kindness. Words and works share the same birthplace and intention when giving comes out of receiving.

8. **Forgiveness of self and others**

   Forgiveness defined: the decision to no longer hold a wrong to someone's account. Receiving and granting forgiveness are traits of maturing individuals who realize that maintaining the load of a wrong committed is a worthless exertion of energy and does severe damage over time to the one who harbors the resentment. Forgiveness when freely granted and received becomes the first point of submission to core values that paves the path to growth.

9. **Treating people with kindness regardless of personality similarities or differences**

There is no substitute for treating people in the same way that one wants to be treated. Yes, it's the Golden Rule. It is especially important that an investment leader openly declares and lives toward a follower in this way.

10. **Demonstrated love**

There is no greater decision than to give one's self away into a candidate who desires to do this for another. When the words of care become consistent life expressions, the authenticity of the investment is never questioned.

Living Proof: "Character-Challenged: Clean It Up"

It was difficult to know where anyone stood with Patrick; while he spoke words that seemed to signify an intent to follow the agreed vision and mission to which the organization had dedicated itself, his actions countermanded his words often enough to cause concern; further, how he presented himself actually denied the validity and, therefore, the viability of his words more times than people could count. Say one thing; practice another. It had become a pattern and was becoming more interwoven into the fabric of the organization to the point that it could no longer be excused or ignored.

If Patrick had been a worker bee, perhaps fewer would have cared, but as a senior VP with authority, position, and power, everyone noticed because it was difficult not to—his station commanded observance, even if true honor and respect for that station was hard to grant, and it was. Some of the managers closest to Patrick simply tried to exempt his blatant dysfunction: "Well, that's just how he is, you know." Others at support levels were offended, and decided to create distance, only dealing with the man whenever job interaction forced such connectivity. Additional staff members were openly aghast as the angst brought on through disconnect between words and actions continued and expanded. It was exacerbated in promises not kept, communication loops not closed, and characters demeaned, whether inadvertent or deliberate. Conversations about this became commonplace; gossip was rampant.

The effects had threaded their ways outside the organization. Damage to image was staggering as suppliers and even customers began to conclude that no one could "count" on Patrick for much of anything—"Make sure that you get what he says you will get before a conversation is over, or you won't get it at all;" at least that was the growing notion.

The problem was worsened in that while people joked about "The Patrick Pass," no one desired or endeavored to confront Patrick about the potential and real negatives of his lack of reliability—except Ed. And Ed was surely an unlikely candidate.

Ed wasn't part of the inner circle of impact, influence or investment; in fact, he was often considered an outsider because his contributions to the firm were made "from a distance," not a physical one as he worked out of an office in the same general location as other staff, rather, from the fact that his department, where he was the maintenance and janitorial supervisor of a staff of two, didn't really appear to be the sector from which a challenge to transgression would come to a senior VP. But it did. And it was about time.

The three maintenance providers had been found faithful in their functions; generally they were "behind the scenes" and therefore not seen or considered much, apart from the accomplishment of recurring duties. There were few complaints about their work ethics or contributions; their credibility generally was high, but their station was low. Still, they were respected. And they overheard everything. In fact, many staffers had used them as "sounding boards" to vent frustrations about Patrick's passing off on commitments during antagonistic conversations where eyes were rolled back and heads were shaken in unbelief.

Ed was in a unique position that allowed him to view with some objectivity the effects of the negative communication about Patrick's action failures. Clearly Patrick's lack of attention to follow-through and closure was wreaking havoc. While the damages that were the products of this continual inconsistency were noticed by virtually everyone, including Patrick's superiors, it took unadulterated courage from the lead of the maintenance and janitorial department to call the spade for what it really was: a shovel that was throwing a lot of dirt around.

Ed had reached a point, like so many others, where he had seen and heard enough. If no one had the courage to tell Patrick the truth, then Patrick would likely bring about more negative results that would only further damage the reputation of the firm. In some community circles that reputation had been tainted already, and was starting to inhibit growth through declines in sales; all because trust was waning, and in some cases absent all together.

Ed thought long and hard, bracing himself for what he was deciding he should do. Often he recalled the "courage" song from one of the characters in one of his favorite movies about following a golden road toward destiny, and he wondered if his courage was sufficient. He laughed nervously to himself when he considered the apparent unreasonableness of him being the one to take the topic home. But he had concluded that the time was now; so, driven by principle and partly by disgust, but mainly by a desire to create something better, this department head started off to see his wizard who was not very wonderful.

The meeting had been scheduled, and Ed had put together an agenda and emailed it to Patrick in advance, consisting of a document called, "Communication Needs: Ways to Improve

Consistency with Services to Staff, Suppliers and Customers."
It felt like a long and verbose title, and it was, but it could serve
to let Patrick know that not all was well, if he would read it.

The day came and so did Ed. Interestingly as the meeting
opened, Patrick thanked Ed for coming forth, said he had
read the agenda, and was concerned about sources of
inconsistency, that it was important something like this be dealt
with, if, as was stated, the effects of not dealing with it were
hurting the firm. He appeared oblivious or willfully ignorant to
any aspect of the dysfunction that could include him!

Speaking first in general terms about the benefits of
matching communication and actions, Ed came to his point
and stated that he (Ed) had observed and concluded that
Patrick often participated in communication that was not
verified by what he did; in fact, the disconnect between his
words and actions when he didn't do anything at all after
promising something in the presence of staff or customers,
was vilifying the company. Ed used three specific illustrations,
rock-solid in their content and context, to illustrate his point;
these included dates, times, names, events, what was said,
and what was not followed up.

Patrick was shocked and, at first, angry as he told Ed that
he (Ed) ought to be fired for disrespect or something like that;
"how dare you"-type comments punctuated the atmosphere
for a time. But Ed stood his ground; both men knew that he
should, and could, because Ed's reputation was noteworthy—
he had earned the right to be heard. Prior to the meeting

there had been some fear as Ed had considered a potential outcome: his being terminated because he dared to cause Patrick to face reality, but Ed had decided that truth telling within a design for overall benefit was worth the risk to him and the organization, so he told the truth, with courtesy and respect.

Patrick fumed, "I hired a caretaker-supervisor, not a psychologist-guru; what possible responsibility do you think you have in telling me that I am the source of any of this?" Ed re-stated his reasons and described again the overall benefits that would accrue if Patrick weighed statements before they were uttered, and once stated, followed through.

Decibels within the meeting peaked and fell as positions were buttressed, facts argued, and outcomes evaluated. Ed had obtained permission from affected persons to use their names specifically in illustrations, and with their advance agreement, to tell Patrick that if so desired, Ed would create a meeting where the full stories from the parties, with the parties present, could be told. "Principle and right practice in cooperation," Ed said, "would change the reality and receptivity of your communication." In other words, if Patrick followed through, people would start to believe him again over time. And they wanted to.

It took more than a week for Patrick to absorb in depth what his physical ears had received in the meeting. Notes taken from the event in combination with the outline Ed had prepared were reviewed. A follow-up meeting then occurred, where Patrick desired to consider further some of what he termed "additional salient points."

The upshot of all this was that within a month Patrick called an assembly of the entire company, including his company president who had been completely disbelieving and disconnected from the whole matter, to deal with the obvious in an up-front way, the degree of which no one, even Ed, could have predicted. The meeting with all 133 staff occurred prior to the opening of the firm on a business day, and every attendee was given an agenda in advance, titled, appropriately, "Communication Needs: Ways to Improve Consistency with Services to Staff, Suppliers and Customers."

In his opening comments, Patrick publicly thanked Ed for bringing an issue to his attention. Few had ever heard that kind of recognition before about anything or anyone from Patrick (at least no one volunteered a memory of it). Patrick then stated that the problem originated with him, Patrick; that he had often said things that he had no intention of aligning with follow-through, not so much out of pre-disposition to harm; instead, a pretending that became placation and then recurrent neglect. Nevertheless, he owned it. And it changed him. Then it changed them.

There was a lot of undoing to undo. Intentionally rectifying damage to intent, inaction and image took careful thought, planning, and execution over months. Not all harm could be fixed, but what could was given best efforts. From the day of the all-company meeting forward, Patrick vouched he would weigh his communication before committing it to words and promises, that pledges would have verifiable time lines, that decisions would be honored. And if mistakes were made, and he stated they probably would be, he would own his errors and asked his employees to own theirs. Not assuring perfection, he did promise perseverance, built upon a sincere apology, an ownership that was heart formed, and a better future his actions would craft.

Leadership owns its faults, positions new actions based on strong alignment of action with core values, communicates these in open forums to those affected, and is accountable to the people that follow.

A pathway for character development is paved where functions align with core values and commitments to strong relationships. Apart from a dedication to "same message" deliverables in function and relationship, there is no accountability, and opportunities for motivating a follower into duplicative leadership will have to wait, if ever they can be constituted at all.

You, as the leader who wants to build strong legacy, will take the challenges of functional responsibility, and see them through to term. You will help a follower reach new heights of attainment to which he or she may aspire by building a model and setting a pace the follower will strive to emulate. You will do whatever it takes if the person and opportunity are right because this is a part of the investment leadership track, and you and your follower are running the track together.

Open Lines of Communication

Communication is possible when more than one person expresses him or herself and someone else is in receiving range. Just because there are two or more people present, however, certainly does not mean communication occurs. Quality investments include a leader's dedication to create avenues of information sharing and truth-telling through fostering atmospheres of openness and completeness. These paths are called "open lines of communication."

Open lines of communication require availability and expressed genuine interest. Assuming and placating don't qualify, nor does glossing over truth. Open communication encourages truth telling in a chosen atmosphere of care and is a demonstration of developing patterns of responsibility where, because people are more important than what they do, the leader and follower listen and engage one another intentionally, and provide space to hear and to be heard.

Open communication certifies that leadership is vulnerable and willing to listen. At least fifty percent of good communication is listening, and there are varying levels of listening from which to choose. Leaders who listen pay attention. Listening that is intentional and dedicated to the person who is speaking is focused. Focused listening by a leader includes providing time for completed thoughts to be expressed, and responses that are comprised of purposeful questions designed to help the follower see truth, respond to truth, and own truth. Open communication is courteous, promotes dignity, and eschews argumentation. It promotes discussion, agreement or disagreement in an attitude of honesty and respect.

Open communication yearns for clarity. A leader and follower thus engaged earn the right and responsibility to act on ideas because they are clearly understood. An investment leader assures clarity before commencing activity, before the run is begun.

Open communication is circular in that it completes its function by returning to the source. A duty or assignment is never totally finished until its task is fulfilled and the person who completed the task confirms to the assignor that full achievement has transpired. Simply put, open communication closes the loops; satisfaction of completeness comes only when they are closed.

One of the investment leader's responsibilities is to show how this is done, literally. Leaders set the examples of the success of follow-through by completing the details. Deliberate dedication to finalizing the small parts is a big part of a determined drive for excellence; open communication assures there is no shirking from any part, or blaming for failure if misunderstanding develops or mistakes occur. Instead, both leader and follower take mutual responsibility to assure that jobs are concluded and communication loops are fully closed.

Open communication produces, or at least contributes heavily to, behavioral change. Action steps demonstrating behavioral change in a verified time line are evidences that communication has taken place. Or, put another way, communication has not fully occurred unless behavioral change follows. These action steps can and should be evaluated consistently, corrected if necessary, and, when success occurs, always celebrated.

Open lines of communication embrace thought patterns that stimulate innovation, permitting people to create and innovate. Freedom of expression is encouraged and unique perspectives celebrated. An idea may have potential to become a great idea until proven otherwise. Great ideas come from solid ideals; open communication stimulates values-driven creativity, thinking "out of the box" in a type of understanding that may include reasonable risk, but always surrounded by the framework of clearly articulated vision, mission, and message.

Open lines of communication allow tough stuff to be faced head on. The investor leader who is working to build long-term legacy is not content with communication that leaves important questions unanswered, nor avoiding responsibility of confronting and dealing with difficult topics. The investor leader endeavors with the follower to fully confront issues and articulate right answers. If the leader doesn't know what the answers are, the leader will commit to locating the answers if they can be found and will often engage the follower in the effort.

Your leadership, if you choose an investment leadership track, will include open lines of communication. If you are passionate about building your legacy, you will declare your wish to communicate in this way, and prepare your followers to respond in like manner, emulating your model.

Cooperative Problem Solving and Conflict Resolution

One of life's common adventures occurs when people have to solve problems together and choose what procedures they will follow when they want to work out the issues, but awaken to the fact that their disagreements discourage or prevent concert of action. Far from being easy, when accomplished well, the investment leader shows a follower who aspires to leadership the way to conquer these challenges by becoming fully involved.

In healthy groups, conflict is not only to be expected, but in some cases encouraged, and only where people's dignity and moral fiber are neither attached nor attacked, and where solutions to problems are creatively designed. In an atmosphere of seeking the best in relationships (decisions) and functions (tasks), conflict may be deemed a needful option as part of the process to achieve a better result. From strong differences of views often come creative thinking and superior solutions. Wholesome conflict is not to be avoided; it is to be handled well. Leaders teach followers how to approach and deal with difficult issues on the basis of core values agreement and character. In a constructive environment, tact replaces being attacked and meaning replaces demeaning. It's a healthy exchange.

There is a process that, when utilized, works well toward resolution of conflict, restoration of relationships, and reconstitution of functions. It works because initial agreements about expectations are in play and participants desire the same goals. Because problems and conflicts are part of life, avoiding them is not a good choice; dealing with them appropriately is, and the process presented here is one way that has proven its effectiveness over and over.

The process is called "Cooperative Problem Solving and Conflict Resolution." It entails five chronological steps and abiding by their sequential order is required. Anyone who wants to know at what point the progress of resolution exists needs only position current action within the chronology to obtain the status and identify the next steps on the way to solving an issue. The steps are not necessarily completed quickly; in fact, some are difficult enough to take a very long time to achieve. It can take a lot of patient work to move from one stage to the next. Further, at each stage, full agreement must be present to allow forward movement.

This process can be applied to help solve virtually any disagreement or problem between people who want to participate in designing and implementing solutions. It is a true test of a leader and follower's desire to grow in interdependence when both parties disagree on some crucial point; how they deal with that disagreement or conflict will show whether the steps form a mere theory of resolution technique or constitute verifiable actions in a powerful process that sees results.

1. **Find the *common ground* of interest and communication…**

   The common ground of interest is the mutually shared reason that triggers the participant's desires to deal with an issue in the first place. Common ground forms the constitution of a solution process and supplies the initial talking points. This beginning step cannot be overlooked. Common ground of interest will be obtained, and the process will be more effective from the outset if initial and across-the-table agreement on identifying the problem, and assurances participants are coming together to engage in answer provision to that problem are firmly established.

   All parties who agree on common interests seek communication in language and forms of expression that are clearly understood by everyone; there shall be no hidden agendas, no off-the-table discussions that are designed to shield a participant from the facts, or cloak the truth behind some kind of spin. The collective decision is to tell the truth.

Further, each participant's dignity is promoted and the worth of each opinion honored. These are the results of efforts to willfully construct what all parties to the discussion deem to be a common ground of interest. In this kind of atmosphere, open communication is fostered as people strive to find and then build on the elements upon which they agree.

2. **For the *common good*…**

   All involved will share in acquired benefits the resolution to the problem will provide, so all parties look to declare what the mutual benefits will be and state them unequivocally. These benefits begin as intangibles, seen as life-lessons to be learned through the process. Tangible rewards follow as parts of steps three and four.

   Writing out the shared benefits is desirable; sharing these with everyone is essential. Some examples may be restored trust, more open communication, positive attitudes, increased commitment, and stronger relationships.

3. **To chart the course for the *common goal*…**

   The leader provides coaching and encouragement as ownership of the process of solution provision is defined and steps for completion are handed out.

Quantifiable expectations are delineated, and action steps to achieve or exceed the expectations are expressed in lists of specific duties and assignments.

The agreement as to the common goal becomes possible to achieve only when the courses to reach the goal are charted within a precise time line where evaluation can mark progress or necessitate changes in course. This stage is one of the most exciting to reach because "seeing the light at the end of the tunnel" creates clarity of thought and purpose-filled action and provides motive and momentum for all who share in the process.

4. **To empower everyone to share in the** *common gains…*

    Tangible rewards come from behavioral change over time. These may constitute wealth or expressions of gratitude, acquisitions of items of value or other forms of gratification, all coming from reaching or exceeding a goal. These gains will come and should be by-products of the intangibles that drive the process on the basis of what is wanted.

5. **To achieve** *uncommon results*!

    Leaders and followers have the right and responsibility to look back on their procedures with healthy pride and an earned sense of accomplishment when this process is followed and resolution occurs. The fifth step is noted as "uncommon" because so many problems are taken to full resolution infrequently; however, when problems are solved in these productive and complete ways, results of the experience in which all participated should be joyfully and gratefully celebrated. Where solution-focused conflict in a group is a mark of health, or where dysfunctional and thorny relational or functional problems have to be handled, the uncommon results of building solutions through this process is a meaningful achievement and worth the efforts.

The key to success in this problem resolution system is the term "cooperative." As the leader, you will help position all parties for winning when you promote cooperation. It's co-operation, and it means that more than one person agrees to contribute to collective participation in an operation based on mutually desired returns. All are engaged in identifying the issues to be addressed, and all are involved at some level in participating in the solutions that are decided. It's a co-operative course. Followers of investment leaders learn how the process works by becoming part of it, and wise leadership looks for opportunities to apply this process when problems arise. This kind of problem solving and conflict resolution goes a long way in helping people see beyond their own needs to the needs of others, an attitude and perspective that are inherent parts of creating legacy.

Living Proof: "Sharon and Karla: The Competition"

Sharon was successful and everyone who networked with her knew it. Not that she was arrogant—she wasn't, but she exuded confidence and held herself like a winner. Throughout Sharon's five-year tenure at the law firm, she had been using facets of investment leadership without really knowing about the name of the concept; trying to help others achieve was "natural" for her. She was happy to learn better methods that she could employ to create added opportunity for success in herself and others, especially where it meant providing clarity in techniques and expected outcomes. Recently she had learned about three leadership tracks and was fascinated with the concept. She wanted to put it to the test.

That opportunity came. With Sharon's rise in popularity came respect and competition. Sharon appreciated competition, especially when she competed with herself to be the best she could be. Her attitude toward competition was one that permitted growth within her and others. However, not all in the firm felt that way about competition. One particular source of competitiveness came from a fellow lawyer; Karla's office was mere feet down the hall from Sharon, and Karla envied Sharon's accomplishments and professional connections and tried to undermine these, covertly at first. As time progressed, some of her practices became anything but subtle or hidden. Crux of the matter: Karla wanted what Sharon had in terms of attention, respect, honor, and reward, and was willing to compete for these by employing tactics that had as their motivation to bring Sharon down a notch or two, or more.

Karla's desires became apparent: hallway and break room conversations with Karla eventually revealed the jealousy. Friends came to Sharon with the obvious and the topic, after awhile, was visited upon Sharon weekly, eventually daily. The atmosphere around these two was becoming thick. While they maintained a business-courteous bearing on the outside, the reality of what was happening on the inside was taking center stage.

While Sharon and her work product were stellar and she knew that Karla's efforts would likely amount to little in real life or alter Sharon's career path, Sharon realized that there was a monkey in their midst. For the respect of each person and the good of the firm in the long run, this sense of unhealthy competition where one person's win was designed to be another person's demise had to be openly revealed and discussed, with the declared goal to create grounds for a solution that would hopefully put negatives behind them and positives before them, so they could support each other regardless of position. It was a tall order.

Sharon took the initiative. In leadership relationship to Karla, Sharon was running on the impact track, and while Sharon did not have positional responsibility over Karla and her output, Sharon wondered if she could approach Karla with enough mutual desire for truth to begin a process of building trust and support. To do this, Sharon decided to talk to Karla about the leadership tracks, to set aside time to leave the office and go on an extended lunch, and begin what could be a process not only of reconciliation but possible investment. The success of the venture at the outset was dependent on Sharon obtaining permission from Karla to even approach what had become a touchy subject for both of them.

Karla consented to lunch and the conversation. This engagement led to others, and communication doors began to open. Karla agreed to be mentored by Sharon on a six-month investment leadership track. Their initial points of interaction required truth-telling, understanding, desire, and explicit permission which Sharon obtained by openly declaring that she wanted the best for Karla and that she, if allowed, would like to have the opportunity to prove it to her.

Leadership seeks opportunities to tell the truth with the other person's welfare in focus. This is especially true when problematic situations are present but have not been dealt with yet. Only with granted permission can a relationship and an investment begin. In this instance, a true friendship was born, and that was an added benefit that neither expected, but both are now relishing.

Creating Realistic Expectations of Results

Unless a finish line is determined, there will be no knowledge of whether or not it was reached after the run is concluded. A realistic expectation is one where the end is clearly defined from the start, and just and compensatory rewards are understood and earned as the processes of goal achievement unfold.

The opposite, of course, is living in unrealistic expectations. These are characterized by vagueness of purpose or ignorance of what counts as goal achievement, murky paths, incomplete actions, and rewards not defined.

If you are the leader who desires to fortify legacy, you will want your followers to live and work in realistic expectations that allow them to know what a win is and how they can reach it. No guessing or gambling with your legacy or their futures. Knowledge of the course and how it concludes is intentional for achieving mutual benefit.

Agreement on results is required when you as the leader, along with your follower, embark on a process of investment. Realistic Expectations are tied to these essentials:

1. **Agreement and adherence to the Code of Achievement, and answers to the Four Questions**
2. **Recognition of Experience:**

    Everyone brings unique experiences to the classroom of life. Experience has brought you to the place you occupy today and taught both leader and follower vital lessons. These lessons, along with core values, help form basics of world-view, character, and worth. Leaders do followers credit when they overtly notice, appreciate and expand upon a follower's experiences and the learning these represent.

A preferred way for a leader to find out what role experience has played in a follower's development is to ask. Then listen. Take note. This follower's experiences are crucial to his or her internal make up, and the leader needs to know them and what values they represent.

3. **Reliance on Education:**

Yearn to learn. The leader pushes learning. In a healthy investment both leader and follower pursue the insatiable desire for knowledge. If that desire is not present, then a leader works to build the hunger for it.

Education takes many forms: formal, continuing, self-starting, degree-enhanced, career-stimulated, or just because a person wants to become more informed. Leaders encourage, if not require, active reading and expansion of numerous educational opportunities in followers who want to grow. When knowledge comes, wisdom shows the "how to" of putting lessons into living, and is the natural and accountable follow-up to expanding education. Leader and follower eagerly undertake this interface.

4. **Review of Environment:**

When, where, and how a person was brought up has profound impact on the development of values and judgment. When you were a child, the choices of environment were made for you. They impact you now. As you grow, you'll review these early causes and effects and weigh their importance.

The adult has to own the responsibility of creating preferred environments every day, and every day those choices are made. A commitment to living in realistic expectations will recognize early impacts, but in addition will drive the follower and leader to choose new environments that form best frameworks into which leadership legacy can be constructed. If an environment is not conducive to promote healthy investment, change it. If it is right, enhance it.

5. **Association with people who stimulate growth and promote health by their examples:**

    A sure and secure investment leader gives confident approval when a follower forms associations with diverse people from whom the follower can learn. Learning doesn't come from a single source. A leader does injustice to the process of development if that leader holds the follower too tightly, excluding other learning options. Leader and follower will agree on structures of association that produce new perspectives, allowing cross-pollination of a variety of ideas.

    One of the hallmarks of maturity is seen in a person's ability to distinguish right from wrong, and judge well what should or should not be considered to be appropriate according to a mutually shared system of core values. Leader and follower seek wiser people from whom to glean greater perspective and understanding, and then decide what to keep and what to discard. Great contributors appreciate, in fact welcome, opportunities to tell their stories and what they have learned from them; students eagerly seek to listen and be taught.

6. **Passion:**

   Passion is the drive that motivates action and comes from a cause that is greater than complacency or comfort. Passion moves a person of diligence to "make a difference." Passion pushes beyond boundaries of isolation, tears down walls of seclusion and erases artificial ease.

   Passion risks because the cause is greater than the cost. Leaders want a follower's passion to build action toward fulfilling realistic expectations. Discovery of passion is to motivation what the heart's pumping is to circulation. Leaders look to ascertain, accentuate and build upon a follower's passion, turning desires into differences.

7. **Season of life and timing:**

   As with the qualifying trials for investment, seasons of life produce time frames in which contributions of significance can take place. Recognizing and responding to "readiness" are integral to determining expectations for success that can truly become reality.

An investment leader intentionally considers seasons in designing and implementing investments that have a chance to win. Leaders and followers use discovery and discussion of season of life as part of setting goals. Integrity from the leader and follower is ingrained into these considerations, because without it, a season can become an excuse to stall or stop. With it, participants learn that a right season provides environments and supports to set actions in place that achieve heart's desires.

8. **Structure:**

Like a building that rises and stands because a sufficient foundation is poured, an investment leader blueprints an organizational grid that positions learning and flexibility while resting on an immovable foundation of principled truth. As the leader, your task is to be certain of the strength of the foundation before you start construction of legacy.

Part of developing structure is the creation of a time line. Investment leadership has a specific start and definitive end; its structure promotes learning within that framework. Evaluation is possible only when a time line is specific. Setting realistic expectations requires putting dates, places and times on a calendar—a place where structures and plans become accountable to each other.

9. **Agreement on communication standards:**

A leader's communication with a follower will reach conclusive proportions when open communication is the rule and not the exception. Achieving consistency in communication requires constant effort from both and is never assumed.

Communication takes effort, and when it breaks down the participants are not content to ignore or sweep issues away in hopes that they won't return. Rather, their diligent commitment to the success of their investment makes them try to communicate again, and again, no matter how long it takes. Living in realistic expectations is a forum where whatever inhibits communication is communicated! Resolution comes when opportunities for dealing with issues in truth replaces abdication or abandonment.

10. **Appreciating personality similarities and differences:**

Much is made of personality. Personality is one of several contributions to an environment motivated by best choices. Too often personality similarities or differences are used as reasons or excuses for varying degrees of ownership and cooperation. Choosing realistic expectations says that the success of engagement is not dependent on, but includes, personality matches and distinctions. Personality doesn't drive, it is driven.

Commitments to behavioral change driven by desire that replaces convenience, affect personality's effects. Personality is subject to commitment. When in its proper place, personality contributes to the process and supports the results a leader and follower expect and toward which they work. Appreciating and incorporating personality similarities and differences are parts of a process of self-control and a mark of maturity.

One of the inherent risks leaders take as they look for followers into whom to pour investment is this: most followers who indicate a desire for this run have insufficient understanding at the outset of the extent and cost to both leader and follower this kind of investment will require. The leader must explain fully what the process entails, the prospects for wins and losses, and how evaluations will be conducted along the way. A leader shows what this process means and entails up-front. Full disclosure is necessary and appreciated.

Your leadership legacy grows in the investment track as the contributions you make to a follower are carried out. The code of achievement, establishing authority and accountability, relational investment, the four questions, nurture and support, functional responsibility, open lines of communication, cooperative problem solving and conflict resolution, and creating realistic expectations of results all contribute to your quality investment and to the passing of the baton.

As you and your follower match stride, you mark progress through evaluation. Quantification helps runners define and celebrate wins, and correct errors, essential functions of running on the investment leadership track.

This is What Leadership Is—
Chapter 5:
Quality Investments

Review and Reinforce:

1. Know, understand and utilize the Code of Achievement: values, vision, mission and message.
2. Properly establish authority and accountability.
3. Pour relational investment into the lives of learners.
4. Ask the Four Questions.
5. Provide functional responsibility.
6. Engage in open lines of communication.
7. Apply cooperative problem solving and conflict resolution for every disagreement, whether in a healthy group or one in which health is waning or absent.
8. Create realistic expectations of results.
9. Appreciate the inherent risks leaders take: that most followers into whom investments are to occur have insufficient understanding at the outset of the extent and cost to both leader and follower this kind of investment will require. Explain the process fully.
10. Your leadership legacy grows in the investment track as the contributions you make to a follower are carried out.

6
Quantifying Tests

Evaluation is a prerequisite to achieving a successful investment. Commitment to it is not an option. To quantify investment leadership's motives, means and ends, the formation of a system of assessments is mandated, period. Running in the investment track is not a casual trot; it is an intentional movement that charts its progress as a legacy is formed.

Assessments look at success-factors and challenge-points of the process often simultaneously. Quantification reviews the worth of the investment by comparing what is desired (the goals) and the achievements (the results) against the principle-driven assemblage of mutually agreed principles (core values).

Your leadership run in the investment leadership track has the opportunity to be duplicated into new people's experiences where the effects of what you and your follower accomplish become models others want to demonstrate. Duplication begins when the evaluation of the current investment shows that success and core values are matching up, and that the investment is being proved reliable. The desire is that new leaders and new followers start their own growth experiences, using your model as a guide.

Creating your model of duplication is a worthy endeavor, and comes about as leader and follower realistically view the wins and struggles of their own investment experiences, tell the truth to those who would come after, simulate and stimulate the regenerative process of people development— because they are a part of it. Active involvement is required. An evaluation system that is working well intentionally applies methods of assessment where correction and readjustment are designed and applied on a recurring basis, and where recognition of the causes for celebration, reward-focused events and future planning occur.

Quantification looks at an investment leader's progress with the follower and sees progression from a "big picture" point of view. This overview helps the runners break their larger perspectives into a collection of important smaller snap shots where they identify failure or success points to empower corrective action or engage in celebrations.

Here is a sample digital photo of the investment track and its key occurrences:

Overview of the Investment Track

1. The beginning of the run is a time when the follower receives information from the leader, sifts it, and sets priorities according to agreed core values, and begins to integrate this information into real life experience.

2. A follower and leader's words and actions are weighed as principles are applied in day to day living.

3. Meeting growth requirements becomes a focus. Felt needs come first, followed by real needs. Real life problems are uncovered and the issues they represent are addressed by shared core values.

4. Intentional learning takes place as problems are solved. Implementing solutions to problems causes behaviors to change.

5. Behavioral change encourages new decisions based on principle; these choices connect to real life situations and have profound effects as maturity increases.

6. Values, vision, mission, and message (the code of achievement) become a standard by which behaviors are measured.

7. Modeling and duplication become possible as others witness changes.

8. A follower's focus turns to outward impact. Learned lessons are taught to observers who may want to do more than observe.

9. Expanding views represent development opportunities

in lives of new individuals whom the follower is called to impact, influence, or into whom investments can occur if agreement is obtained and the timing is right.

10. Success and succession form a transferable life-model, the baton is passed, the follower becomes the leader, and the investment begins all over again in the life of another. Legacy is won.

Investment leadership is a continuing paradigm and includes several stages of progress that occur simultaneously. Growth patterns are constantly evaluated as results are reproduced into the lives of others.

Consistency of focus is required in this reproducible model. A leader within any of the three tracks weighs when and where to move with a follower so that best results come from expended effort.

Evaluation is absolutely necessary to assure that the decisions a leader and follower make are right and are made at the right time. Energy and time are not wasted; they are applied with purpose and diligence.

Living Proof: "Stan, Stacey and Their Production Teams"

A career in aerospace consumed the energies of two competent leaders. Stan began as a team participant on one of Stacey's project groups. It didn't take long for Stacey to see his potential, not only as a follower who contributed to a superb work product, but also as a potential leader who could and probably should at some point lead his own team.

When Stan joined the team initially he was unknown, except for a résumé that helped position him with responsibility at a junior level. The team was new with many participants unacquainted with each other. The game of "waiting to see if they all would make the grade" caused settling in to take longer than any really wanted. As goals brought about more deadlines and new contracts ushered in extended hours to bear on planning and production, tempers occasionally grew short, and no one at this point was thinking much about building relationships. They had jobs to do.

Stacey wanted to be a good leader and had learned of three leadership tracks. She saw herself as an impact leader to many, and an influence leader to her specific team which consisted of fifteen people. Even though extremely busy in the requirements of her production schedule, she scanned her impact and influence horizons. She floated the possibility with her VP of creating two teams out of one to increase production. This was doable if new and solid leadership could be developed and resources to accomplish this were allocated. While the benefits of duplication were clear, the process did not appear to be easy. Regardless, Stacey determined that results would outweigh costs, and received approval to proceed with plan development.

First order of business: create a new model of output,

where the numbers would speak for themselves. She understood that this aggressive approach demanded another competent leader be found and trained. It took many hours of solo engagement for Stacey to create a plan that would withstand close scrutiny. She prepared it well, and presented it well, and was given the go ahead to launch a new team. Much, if not most, of the success of this team depended on her new leader's capability, the development of whom would be Stacey's responsibility.

Stacey and Stan had worked together well, and Stan was present on the day when Stacey publicly announced the plans that had been approved to find the ways to produce more by dividing and conquering. Stacey explained openly that she was looking to build leadership that would become the capstone of the success of the new team. She told everyone that anyone who wished to apply for this position should do so by an imposed date and dismissed the meeting.

It was only a half hour later when Stan appeared at her door, having been encouraged to apply by at least seven other team members! His potential was seen from above, across and beneath, and he wanted an opportunity to grow.

As they spoke, Stacey emphasized that from a position and influence perspective he would certainly be a candidate for leadership of the new project team. But she wanted to know if Stan wanted to consider becoming a follower in her leadership investment track, and described what the components would look like. One of the central focus points would be Stan's desire to not just grow in influence but in impact on a larger audience as this team became known, that Stan would look for opportunities like Stacey had to pour his knowledge into a "little Stan" if one could be found.

The agreement and investment produced a new leader, a new team, and raised production by 33% in the first three months of implementation. Stan's impact grew to the point that Stacey's supervisor and his team approached both Stacey and Stan about setting up leadership training courses for people who had "potential." The results were speaking for themselves.

Cycles of impact, influence and investment leadership continue and form a repeating pattern.

If you desire to put your leadership up to the quantification tests, realize that evaluation will examine your leading and your follower's learning. It will show areas of wins you should celebrate, and points of loss you should correct. Leadership on this track of investment is visible and open to inspection, as will be the legacy your leadership will create.

Quantification processes are a collection of methods that are not all that complex; but to be effective they must be consistently applied for the truest pictures to emerge. Here are several considerations that help the quantification system succeed: Motives and Methods of Correction and Realignment, Celebration, and Future Planning.

Motives and Methods of Correction and Realignment

When a leader and follower engage in teaching and learning together, victories will occur and mistakes will be made. It is important to learn from both. From victories, learn what constituted success and duplicate it. From failures, learn what to avoid, replacing negative with positive.

Regular correction and readjustment are standard acts in quantifying impact, influence or investment leadership. Evaluations are regularly integrated into patterns of activity and expected results. True vision points up areas requiring realignment, points of high fulfillment, and the celebrations that are parts of these honored achievements.

Evaluations are objective and subjective at the same time. They are objective in that they approach accomplishment from the outside in, weighing whether function is working; they are subjective in that they consider from the inside out whether internal relationships are growing as parts of a process of maturing.

Evaluation requires the follower be in possession of his or her own progress, while at the same time receiving teaching and coaching from the leader. Because the leader is more committed to relationship development than function fulfillment as a priority, the leader's coaching seeks to show by word and example that functional fulfillment, proper ownership, and the accomplishment of realistic expectations with excellence are all driven by highly valued moral and relational standards. The leader sets this balance in place and perseveres in the creation of the model.

Evaluation procedures are conducted with specified agendas, clearly stated goals and prospects for future wins. These procedures are driven by the need for authenticity and become examples of truth telling in an atmosphere of dedication to the welfare of another.

Evaluations should culminate in specific action steps over a declared time frame to enhance production and build the person. These action steps are integrally designed to produce the holistic results a follower and leader desire.

Evaluations are opportunities to see how relationships and functions are cooperating together and are being reinforced within personal impact, influence or investment tracks. Because relationships precede and give definition to function, evaluations are conducted with the person in mind first, and the product, or function, second. As strong relationships develop, quality of function is viewed as vital, not optional; excellence is sought after; accountability is high.

In correct alignment with relationship, proper transfer of ownership of function occurs as right relationships are modeled and taught. Function with excellence is the child of strong relationships. Because a leader knows that the decision to begin an investment relationship constitutes a decision to pour into the success of another, excellence of function on the part of the follower becomes the verifiable result that the leader's relational investment is working.

Quantifying an investment shows the context and content of the quality of relationship and fulfillment of function that healthy relationships generate. The ties between relationship and function are strong; the means (relationship and function in balance) and the ends (results) match in an investment leadership run that is preparing to pass the baton, following the code of achievement. Evaluations see the activity (function), ask the why (reasons/values) behind the action, and define how (the methods) the process of development (relationship) is affecting choices (the lessons) and generating life models and legacy (the result).

A potential risk is that evaluations can be seen as intimidating to a follower, or their results used to put down and discourage a follower from continuing his or her efforts to win. An investment leader does not use intimidation; it is not even considered. There is simply no room for power plays, positional arrogance or selfish ambition when an investor leader seeks to build legacy in the investment track.

Quantification will include facing failures up front and providing corrective activity—these are simply part of the run of growth. Care about the condition of the follower, especially on the heels of failure or in the midst of struggle should not prevent the leader from telling the truth to a follower whose need is to hear it; rather, the leader judges what the correct time will be when a follower's receptivity is highest and the potential for progress is greatest. In an attitude of consideration of the other's welfare, the leader decides on the context and presentation of content so that truth may be well received and corrective action steps implemented. Right attitudes, right words, right action, right timing: all of these are part of the quantification tests.

Ten Questions to Help Stimulate Quantification Discussions

Using the ten questions below can help stimulate quantification discussions, but this is only a template—alter and adjust to make them right in your leadership application. Regardless of the exact form of the questions, the more specificity that is used, the better the understanding.

In preparation to asking these, leader and follower must agree that evaluation is a necessary procedure and is designed to benefit, not belittle or corner. Pure motive of application should not become an impediment to quality interaction; give and take should be present. Real life engagement is the goal.

If you are the leader, make sure you personalize these questions and their answers for yourself and with your follower:

1. What am I learning?
2. How am I applying what I am learning in day-to-day experience?
3. What results am I seeing?
4. What corrections do I need to make because of the results I observe?
5. How am I celebrating successes?
6. Who is being impacted from my life's model?

7. What do I still need to learn?
8. What are the next steps in my learning process?
9. When and where will I engage in the next learning steps?
10. How are my tasks and my desires for excellence in accomplishing them (functions) supporting the authenticity of the decisions I have made (relationships) and the reasons (values) behind my decisions?

A regular time should be set aside where leader and follower engage in evaluation questions, answers, and discussions they produce. Calendaring these sessions is the only way to assure they will occur. Be sure that when the time is right the participants are ready. Make the environment conducive; fewer interruptions allow a more thoughtful discussion to ensue.

An evaluation procedure is a precursor to passing the baton. Remember that perfection is not the goal; perseverance in matching real life with the code of achievement is. When you as the investment track leader and your follower are engaged in quantification, you are qualifying yourself and your follower to prepare to pass the baton, and putting together a living legacy. Truth in evaluation and the actions that follow are the worthwhile parts of this run.

Celebrations

You will win; so will your follower who is matching your stride. When you do, celebrate. Leaders know the value of wins and congratulate progress in various ways throughout the process. Leaders who build legacies comprehend worth of ongoing recognition. Leader and follower understand, because it has been communicated many times and in many ways that leadership is constantly looking for a follower's daily causes to celebrate, regardless of size.

Leaders itch for a triumph, are "on the watch" to catch their people in the act of doing things well and notice them, right then! In a work world environment, inspiring leadership is demonstrated often as a leader roves, "stopping by" a follower's location to "check in," offering praise as a project is seen in developmental phases, or providing assistance. The thrust here is noticing! An investment leader's attention to detail as a follower's success story unfolds demonstrates genuine interest, and provides opportunities for affirmation.

Causes for celebration are observed quicker when relationships are strong and communication procedures are active. If you as the leader haven't seen many successes in your follower lately, how much of the cause of this oversight comes from a lack of relational connectivity?

Right when the good things are happening is the time that the causes for celebrations should be written down, filed and remembered, or immediately praised, and will be when the connectivity points are strong. The quality of relationships can never be assumed; it's consistently reinforced, and always appreciated; committed leaders work at it, and see many chances for celebration as they do.

Some successes simply can't wait for a company or department party to be the place of recognition, so have a "party" at the moment of affirmation; be prepared to provide instant recognition. Celebrate accomplishments with notes, cards, email messages, verbal "Thank-you!" expressions, affirmations in front of a follower's peers or in the presence of other leadership, smiles and direct eye contact, appropriate touches, phone calls, lunches, dinners, dances, theater and concert tickets, get-a-ways, sports tickets, gift certificates, books, subscriptions, CDs, videos, video games, time off, retreats, extended holidays… the list could go on.

Spontaneous celebration can be its own reward and can reap its own lasting results in new efforts and innovation from the one being recognized. The effects of the encouragements in these smaller moments can last a lifetime. Celebrations are mini-investments within themselves. In healthy relationships, celebrations create opportunities for more to come—much like a boomerang, they return whenever they are tried. The results are contagious. Celebrations also go both ways and are not limited by titles, places or positions. Followers should congratulate and celebrate the leader for a win. In fact, the leader needs this praise, and great leaders accept it with genuine thanks.

Giving and receiving affirmations are true expressions of a person who is maturing. A follower or leader who says that he or she likes to give affirmation but doesn't need to receive it may or may not be living in truth; certainly if the person means it, it indicates that affirmations of success don't play nearly the role they should in the building of the person. One who says that affirmation is a gift that can be given but need not be received simply is not balancing the worth of an individual with the contributions they make.

Giving and receiving are part of the same operation, of course, so look for chances to give affirmation, and gratefully receive it when it is presented to you. Let creative impetus grow for those special and interesting ways of saying and hearing, "I appreciate you; you have done well."

Celebrations of success can come in many forms, and sometimes it is challenging to pick the right one for the person or circumstance. One way of finding out what kinds of celebrations people enjoy is to ask them. Then, remember what they have said and create those celebration moments, whether spontaneous or long-term planned, that mean the most to the recipients.

Effective leadership utilizes many innovative ways of celebrating relational and functional achievements. The act of doing so is born from a commitment to recognize others as they run to win and genuinely affirm them when they do, knowing that this dedication leads to greater people accomplishing greater things. Celebrations produce their own little legacies whenever they take place, so leaders and followers set their tones and create their environments that yearn to be filled with celebratory expression. Let the parties begin! You're invited.

Future Planning

Planning ahead is one of many indicators of balanced relational and functional health. It is a necessity when leadership investment is committed to applying no-change principles into ever-changing environments. Strength is seen when leaders and followers take enduring views of completing short-term and long-term goals on their investment leadership track, make the time to plan accordingly, and follow through on their plans.

Leader and follower work together on planning for the future. When they do, complacency in an attitude of "Having arrived, I need go no further…" is not tolerated or even contemplated. Coming on the heels of celebrating, planning directs the focus to brand new vistas, as part of building legacy.

Leaders in all three tracks learn from experiences—disappointments and victories—and keep their eyes on innovating for the future. Past lessons encourage future planning to include the "what if…" creative paradigms of thinking. Future planning risks, seeks reward, and will not be sidetracked by temporary setbacks.

Leadership's initiatives are driven by ever-present golden opportunities to "find a better way" and "build better people." Challenge and change, opportunity and action, are partners in planning for the future.

Challenge and change, opportunity and action, are partners in planning for the future.

Investment leadership in particular strives to encourage followers to see fresh and unique perspectives with broad and goal-directed vision, holistically. This visionary view on the future becomes task sensitive as action steps are defined and refined, and bigger and long-term goals are broken up into bite-sized pieces of short-term achievements. A perspective on the future anticipates simultaneously relational and functional successes; failing to plan can indeed mean planning to fail with both. An optimistic attitude and pro-activity replace predispositions for failure as leader and follower look to the future and lean into it.

Investment leadership and its leader on the run, move forward while learning from the past, fulfilling its present with the presence of quality relationships and functional accountability. A leader and follower have a great commission to fulfill; planning for the future assures their future will not become a great omission. When they are intentionally committed to values-driven future planning, they will promote a balance of relationship and function, setting up movements for heightening leadership's effectiveness as they both mature, producing new and transferable models. More on this in Chapter 10, "Action Steps."

Your job as the investment leader is to assure sufficient time is set aside for overview, evaluation, correction, celebration, and future planning. Accomplishing these quantification procedures with your follower is part and parcel of preparing to pass the baton of legacy.

This is What Leadership Is—
Chapter 6:
Quantifying Tests

Review and Reinforce:

1. Evaluation is essential.
2. To quantify investment leadership's motives, means and ends, the formation of a system of assessments is required.
3. Active involvement in evaluation is required of both investment leader and follower.
4. An overview helps to see the process of investment with a "big picture" focus, so that smaller segments of wins and losses can be placed in proper perspective.
5. When a leader and follower engage in teaching and learning together, victories will occur and mistakes will be made. It is important to learn from both.
6. Evaluations are objective and subjective at the same time.
7. Evaluations are opportunities to see how relationships and functions are cooperating together and are being reinforced within the impact, influence or investment tracks.
8. Function with excellence is the child of strong relationships.

9. Use personalized questions and discussion formats— real-life engagement is the goal.

10. Causes for celebration occur as investment relationships unfold and tasks are completed together: these are the wins. Use creative celebration methods; let the parties begin!

11. Planning ahead is one of many indicators of balanced relational and functional health.

12. Your job as the investment leader is to assure sufficient time is set aside for overview, evaluation, correction, celebration, and future planning. Accomplishing these quantification procedures with your follower is part and parcel of preparing to pass the baton of legacy.

7

Creating Leadership Models that Work

A "model" can be described as an inanimate object, artificial copy or replica of some kind. And while these definitions are partly true within the meaning of the word, they are void of life. In the investment leadership discussion, "model" is used differently. A "model" is a living entity, whom in character and condition illustrates the cause and actualization of relationships; where participants willingly decide and adopt principles and corroborating actions in environments they create, that foster consistency, thrive on integrity, earnestly seek excellence, and duplicate their effectiveness over time by investing in others of like passion, so that the product of the original is greater than the original itself.

The results of life-legacy leadership on the investment leadership track are seen in a follower's contributions that will be greater, perhaps in scope, size, span or scale than the leader's initial investments into the follower's experience alone. Further, this model produces positive and recurring effects through the follower's investment into others, because it is not limited to the follower's improvements alone. In fact, investment leadership's success is truly accomplished when a follower of your follower becomes a new leader of new followers, and begins his or her own investment track run.

Finishing and Finishing Well

If you are the leader running in the investment leadership track, you are committed to finding and developing followers who have the potential and desire to win and to duplicate. In this model, those that would emulate it assure the future and make possible the continual passing of the baton. The differences between "finishing" and "finishing well" provide a description of this working model's success.

"Finishing" is what impact, influence, or investment leadership may accomplish when the follower shares the leader's example, has learned the means of leading, and exercises improved and core-values-based impact or influence on people in his or her expanding network—a first level success, and not at all something to be discredited. Heavy on agreement and activity, but light on legacy.

"Finishing well" is when extraordinary investment leadership has been so invested that a follower moves from his or her impact and influence leadership tracks into leadership that intentionally invests in another, and is only satisfied when that investment is replicated into and within an additional life—this is second-level investment which duplicates and guarantees the success of the first. This investment leadership model demands and settles for nothing less than a regenerating outcome where the reproduction of values occurs within next generations. Results within this paradigm are exponential in their effectiveness, and broadly affect lives for the better in quantitative as well as qualitative measures.

Too many leaders settle for one-level finishes, which in the course of time puts a period on the construction of their life's legacy sentence, even though the follower and leader may be gratified in the process. Duplication's life sentence simply doesn't end; it is for all time punctuated with a semi-colon or comma; it keeps on providing truth's context, content, and meaning. Your long-term legacy's creation demands that you finish well. A leadership model that works and finishes well will have two tenets of action: Constructing a Value System and Mentoring for Life Change.

Constructing a Value System

A leader's expectations of a follower and a follower's expectations of a leader share common values: concrete fundamental principles of life beliefs and living practices. A value system is a collection of these core values, but the system is more than a list. In aggregate the core values form a composite framework of principles that taken holistically provide measurements against which atmospheres, attitudes and actions can be evaluated as to how they measure up in practice and outcomes when compared to the standards of the system.

A value system integrates right principles with right practices in the assurance that empowered and changed behaviors will produce better and more positive results. Principles, processes and production (motive, means and ends) are all considered and weighed within a value system. The system is dynamic in that while it is based on unchanging truths, it continually adjusts its means according to the needs of the culture in which it is applied (work, family, and social environments). The system is resoundingly strong, resilient in nature, responsible in practice, but not rigid in method.

A value system when operational, empowers a leader and follower to grow while they are engaged in the practices of their investment. It is vital that both leader and follower are committed to fulfilling and abiding by the core values to which they willfully commit themselves when they create and implement their value system.

Establishing a value system is the first action step in creating an investment model that works toward preserving and expanding legacy, and is a necessary part of running in the investment leadership track. Initial agreement on the composition and use of the values within the system is not an option; indeed it is a singular preparation to accomplishing success.

Opportunities for success are magnified where agreed values form the cornerstone of this enterprise. An investment leader knows the importance of core values, and with the follower, creates a list of these that will be validated and ratified by both. Upon ratification, their values list provides the grid that measures the quality of their relationships (their decisions about each other's successes) and the excellence of their functions (actions that illustrate and validate those decisions). This grid becomes the standard for attitude and behavior. Shared dedication to perseverance of the standard elicits motives and desires. The system also allows that when failures come, and they will, the next exercise will be ownership, and forgiveness that is granted and received.

Twelve Laws of Understanding

The "Twelve Laws of Understanding" below make up a value system for the reader's consideration. A leader and follower may of course constitute their own system and form of presentation; regardless, their shared activity of creating and then ratifying such a system is one necessary step for leading and following to be effective and transferable. The more participatory involvement leader and follower share in its construction, the more opportunities for ratification and implementation the participants own.

The "Twelve Laws of Understanding" are laws about life and principles about living that are born out of growing understandings of fundamental truths that are as old as the rule of law for desired good. For ease of reference, the laws are listed first; then listed again with commentary. The Twelve

Laws are also found at the end of the book in a smaller font should you desire to produce a wallet-sized photocopy. Learn them, live them; when they are alive in you they will change lives in measurable ways, including yours, and become examples of truth enfolded into deeds—the passing of the baton, and the living of a legacy.

Twelve Laws of Understanding

1. Realize I am responsible for my own choices, not others'; that changing someone else's behavior is not my responsibility; rather, I need to change me.
2. Seek to understand how the other person thinks and communicates; use his or her language.
3. Model what I want.
4. Set realistic limits on what is acceptable behavior.
5. Impose these limits on myself, first.
6. Desire the best, but prepare for difficulty; seek creative, peaceful solutions.
7. Seek and pray for wisdom.
8. Remember, at the right times.
9. Encourage always.
10. Think first, listen most, and speak seldom.
11. Realize growth involves change, change can mean pain, and patience on the journey is a virtue.
12. Love. Establish meaningful relationships.

Twelve Laws Commentary

1. **Realize I am responsible for my own choices, not others'; that changing someone else's behavior is not my responsibility; rather, I need to change me.**

   "It's all about me" applies here, but in a different context than what that phrase normally represents. Here this means that the leader takes responsibility, first.

   Change originates with the leader, not the follower, and evidences the leader's submission and obedience to agreed principles and practices. Willful change on the part of the leader teaches followers how to follow as a precursor to instructing them how to lead. A leader cannot "own" a follower's choices to change; the leader's job is to define through his or her actions the examples of what constitutes good choices and their consequences when behavioral change occurs.

2. **Seek to understand how the other person thinks and communicates; use his or her language.**

   Communication becomes possible when a common language is spoken and received. This is about more than just words or dialect, of course; this meaning speaks to the participant's desire to understand another's thought-patterns based on mutual worldviews from established principles, and how best these are communicated in form and function.

W.O.R.D.: Communication has occurred when verifiable behavioral changes follow. If a leader truly desires change-behavior communication, the leader makes diligent efforts to learn how the follower thinks through observance of the follower's words and deeds and through sharing ideals and ideas at deeper levels of conversation—conversation dwelling at depths where a "word" is represented by W.O.R.D.: defined as Worthwhile (based on core values), Observable (seen in action), Reliable (duplicative), Declarations (clear and acknowledged pronouncements).

3. **Model what I want.**

The leader sets the pace, creates the duplicative model, and then teaches the follower how to receive what the model offers, and thereby achieves more than the model-maker perhaps ever envisaged. The term "model" can be used as a noun and a verb, and understood as a state and an action. Results that illustrate exponential growth and personal behavior may be seen in its "double" interpretation.

4. **Set realistic limits on what is acceptable behavior.**

Some behaviors are not acceptable: those that violate shared and agreed values; those that destroy others for the sake of power and position; those that stifle; those that inflict pain for damage's sake; those born of deceit; those that violate trust in a relationship; those where forgiveness and restitution are thwarted by need for excessive control and intimidation; those that come from an "end justifies the means" way of living where production comes at the unnecessary, unlawful, or heedless sacrifice of people and what they represent; those where worth is measured only in the amount of benefits a leader obtains; and those where manipulation and delegation stand in the way of development of mentoring and deputizing (more on this below). Defined and unalterable limits are set for these undesirable behaviors and they are replaced with their opposites.

Acceptable behaviors are eagerly supported: those that share agreed core values; those that build others up regardless of power and position; those that encourage; those that promote healing; those born of truth; those that prove trust; those where forgiveness and restitution are actively employed when errors are made; those that value people and process more than end-production; those that celebrate follower's wins; and those where mentoring and deputizing are the rule.

5. **Impose these limits on myself, first**.

The leader purposefully integrates limits on his or her behavior, defining what is acceptable according to an agreed value system and the principles that place people first. The leader takes the initiative and behaves in the ways he or she wants others to behave. This initial and intentional imposition to manage one's personal behavior is proof positive of a leader's control of self, and the desire to serve as a model-maker.

This healthy control validates the leader's people-first orientation, and encourages behaviors that are not only acceptable, but also desirable and appreciated by those who follow.

6. **Desire the best, but prepare for difficulty; seek creative, peaceful solutions.**

Circumstances change, character shouldn't. In fact, character should become stronger in an investment leader when circumstances challenge the validity of its nature. Character makes ready for the worst while it dwells on innovating for the best.

Leaders engaged in investment strategies may find themselves at points of disagreement or confrontation. These can contribute to growth whenever they occur— confrontation constructs when it is rightly framed. One who would build a lasting legacy sees beyond the present difficulties to the lessons that can change lives, and seeks solutions that point the way to those successful conclusions.

The leader who lives for more than immediacy tries through strength of character to make peace when circumstances beyond one's control present challenges not anticipated. This leader recognizes the reality of problems, but with a positive outlook and a focus on the greater benefit, offers solutions, and confronts negatives with what is desired above and beyond the dysfunction.

Sometimes the leader elevates his or her initiative and uses force when the higher call takes preeminence over what may be politically correct, usually acceptable, or on the surface preferred. If evil encroaches, the commonly shared values of character, the desires for tranquility and the freedom to grow will compel the use of needed, lawful, appropriate and available methods, to overcome someone else's ill intent to destroy that which is right and good.

7. **Seek and pray for wisdom.**

    Great leaders know that as part of their chosen make-up they must continue to be learners of principle and practitioners in truth. Wisdom—applied knowledge—comes from diverse sources. How many times these leaders seek wisdom from those who have gone before and through prayer or deep contemplation will often be signals of the degree of healthy dependence these leaders have on reliable "others" who serve as teachers and model-makers. Great leaders are bold in their search for models through which and from whom they learn.

8. **Remember, at the right times.**

    In the heat of the moment is when memory of what is right and how best to express it often fails, or seems to. But it is in those times when remembering and doing the right things should become the "natural" responses even though by common standards they may not be "normal."

Remembering in crucial times originates from repetitive practice within prior mind-sets, when learning appropriate responses comes from lived examples and experiences, over and over. Rehearsal is part of preparing for reality; leaders are rehearsed, prepared, and positioned to remember.

9. **Encourage always.**

Confidence shared is conviction that cares. Encouragement comes from security of personhood, experience and perspectives that identify with another's life encounters, and offers clarity and assurance that "this, too, shall pass." It shows that when life's circumstances are passed through well, maturity results.

Encouragement becomes a naturally borne habit when it comes from strong relationship-connection points (when one has made good decisions about another's success). Its opposite, of course, is discouragement, seen as an impediment to growth, and it usually originates from attitudes of threat, intimidation, fear, isolation or abandonment.

Encouragement is conquering negative circumstances with fortitude, certainty, boldness, connectivity and engagement born of dwelling in principle instead of cowering in panic. A leader who is secure will joyfully and tactfully share tracks to wellness for the benefit of another's welfare.

10. **Think first, listen most, and speak seldom.**

Those who are most knowledgeable will have acquired their station by positioning themselves as students most of all. Leadership that seeks to invest in another must learn to think before reaching conclusions, listen prior to offering solutions, and speak only when there is something clearly important to say.

In chronological order, these three follow each other naturally when applied consistently. Caution, as part of a process, or timing to consider another's person and position carefully first, listen intently and then declare intentionally, is a component of purposed self-control—here a precursor to assure that what a leader says is consistent with what needs to be said for the follower's benefit.

11. **Realize growth involves change, change can mean pain, and patience on the journey is a virtue.**

Change of conduct characterizes genuine developing maturity. Behavioral change occurring within healthy relationships is not accidental; it is forethought, anticipated, and planned.

Its implementation can mean pain when it issues

from life's university of knocks and nicks. People involved in learning the tough lessons require understanding and compassion from an investor leader who is running with a follower through the process.

An investment leader building legacy is aware that there will be times when marked change points in a follower's experience will occur, predicts them prior to their arrival if possible, and certainly identifies them as they transpire. Struggle is predictable when a person decides to change for the better. As learning becomes living, knowledge replaces ignorance, and efforts born of wisdom replace excuses born of whining; the investment leader demonstrates patience, care, and compassion toward the follower who is weather-beaten or needs a break.

Forms of demonstrating patience will vary, of course; but they never smack of anything other than genuine interest in the success of another through positive, up-front and others-focused attitudes, words and actions.

12. Love. Establish meaningful relationships.

Of all the models of love that are known, none is stronger than that which gives up everything for the benefit of another. This love knows that its giving will cause life change in both giver and receiver.

Relationships become meaningful when the process of growing them means giving fully for the advantage of one who will receive. "Love, to be love, must be given away," says the lyric in a song by my good friend, the late David Hopkins, and it's true. Love is not a state of being; it's an action word, working its character in and through the context of another person's life for their good.

Leaders who decide to run in the investment track find their choices to love are costly; but they will choose love as a cornerstone of legacy regardless, because it's right. Within followers who receive its merit, their acceptance and application of love alters lives in remarkable and measurable ways from that moment on. They simply have to give it away to somebody else.

The power of a shared value system is undisputed. Within the investment leadership track, where agreed values are founded on high morals and principles, you as the leader will seek to elevate the individual through the demonstration of your character's quality, and provide for best results consistent with desired good. This combination is a formidable force for positive contributions, and they always begin with the leader.

Living Proof: "Environmental Concerns"

The working environment for management and line staff at the relief center headquarters was anything but pleasant.

Not only were roles and responsibilities undefined and there-fore confusing, attitudes from senior leadership were conde-scending, placating and sometimes down right rude. Visitors may never have seen this mess; indeed the contributions this organization made to needy populations' centers contributed to an image of internal health, but the trappings of the image were merely what outsiders and recipients thought they saw. Inside there were grave and growing problems.

Some staffers wondered why they even continued to stay and work in these unproductive personnel and work environments. When those questions arose in conversation, they were usually answered with, "I guess because I believe in the cause. I want to make a difference, and in spite of the problems here, I stay to do the best work I can and forget senior staff." Growing gossip and negativity were perpetuated by disconnect; no matter the resilience of some, a few of the "old-timers" had said that they had experienced enough and were floating résumés. A few had already left in disgust and had said, "Good riddance!" to the company.

Leadership at the top appeared to be a primary source of dysfunctional relationships that forced creation of an employee façade, trying to show outward commitment in spite of internal strife. Staffers had repeatedly approached a senior manager, Olivia, to "Do something!" but this leader felt her hands were tied. Olivia believed in the community and charitable purpose for which they all worked and felt she could be more effective within the organization than out of it; but in her position, she feared real recrimination if she were to take staff complaints "up" to top leadership and the likely loss of her job if she was to confront the CEO.

James was not new to the CEO's position. He had served in this capacity for nearly six years. Some initial successes brought deserved perks, and before too long, pride, along with the approval of a well appointed board of directors, seemed to assure his contentment and continuance. He was the boss, the authority figure, and he put people in their places if need be to assure his positional clout. He possessed no hesitation when moving a subordinate who did not agree with him. He promoted divisional competition that led to mistrust and backstabbing. Sectional "class-views" framed a working surrounding in which intimidation was used as a tool to solidify authority and power.

Appreciation coming from James was unheard of; he often said that because he didn't need it, his managers probably didn't either. Rebuke when mistakes were made was the recognition they received. James seemed to pride himself in being difficult to know or understand. In spite of this, Olivia believed that James was sincere in his declared belief in and support of the cause. But providing help to others externally while showcasing disrespect internally was inconsistent behavior and sent a mixed message that was becoming more and more unbelievable.

Time after time, Olivia saw James demean or talk down to his employees with unbounded sarcasm. Some of these folks were members of her staff. A few of her quality people had come to her with mounting complaints born of growing anger, frustrations and weariness with it all. Olivia cherished unity and wanted to promote it, but unity was becoming virtually impossible in this environment where James's behavior continued to be unmoved by the needs of his own staff and organization.

The situation reached a crisis point when James berated one of Olivia's staff for what appeared to be a minor but recurring infraction in front of other staff. Hurtful words were spoken and embarrassing negative attitudes and actions permeated the room and infected the people. In the opinion of many, total disregard was demonstrated from both sides. When attacked, the employee had answered James with extreme disrespect to the point where James, in front of everyone, yelled back and told the employee to leave—and he fired him. The employee departed in anger, but not without letting everyone in ear shot know what he thought of James; acting in ways unseemly and uncalled for no matter the source of the conflict. The scene had gotten out of control.

Olivia's first reaction was to try to "make it better," but this one couldn't be made better, at least not then. Days following the employee's public and disruptive departure, Olivia decided that James, who had made no appearance since that time into her area, had to be confronted with truth about the damage done. It was a tough decision for her to choose to be the bearer, and one she felt that although was right, was going to be very difficult to follow through.

To break a negative cycle, Olivia decided to try methods that James had not used. Her focus became creating a new atmosphere that Olivia knew she would likely be solely responsible to facilitate. Determining the approach she would employ to talk to James and what to say to this man were scary thoughts as she pondered and planned. It was obvious the dismissed employee had not been producing excellence and that mistakes were repeatedly made; it was also obvious that James's behavior was inappropriate no matter the condition of the employee's work product. Many who witnessed this main event considered the blow up to originate from James's consistent disapproval and lack of appreciation of people in general, that his brusqueness had brewed itself into something much stronger in an environment that most dreaded, to some degree anyway, and which many felt he had manufactured in the first place. In other words, it was his creation and his fault.

While she considered how to implement her decision to confront, Olivia became acquainted with three leadership tracks and decided to design the context and content of her meeting with James through her growing understanding of what the tracks represented and how to lead within them.

While James certainly had leadership position and influence, his overall impact on many was small and any chance for investment erased because of his isolated focus and belittling nature. Olivia, in contrast, had witnessed her own leadership impact growing; many felt she was moved to act on principle and her influence gave her a platform on which to approach James. So now eyes were on her. How she accomplished this task of confrontation could reap great rewards; she thought that she might find potential for new investment opportunities if she was successful, but into whom at this point she didn't know.

Her goal became: Do the right thing in the right way to achieve the best results. In her preparation, she learned that leadership's responsibility was to engage in cooperative problem solving and conflict resolution. She began to look for common ground of communication and interest with James, common good, common goals, and common gains, and wondered what her uncommon results would be. She certainly wanted to keep her job, but more importantly she wanted to position the company for internal growth that no one had seen, yet.

The approach she chose included requesting permission to meet with James and designing and sending an agenda to him in advance. She composed the following communication:

Dear James:

In support of our mutual commitment to fulfill the cause of the company, I would like to explore ways of staff conflict resolution with you that I believe have the potential of across-the-board ownership of solutions that will result in more efficient job completion, as well as better working environments.

Several challenges face us now since the departure of William. From a desire to make our company stronger on the inside I want to address these with you in a solution-minded manner. With your permission, when we meet I will bring two problem-answering game plans for you to weigh on the merits of what they can accomplish. Both will be focused on building productivity and fostering high morale. Both are financially responsible; in fact, they will cost little if any money. They will require agreement for implementation from all leadership: managerial and above.

Thanks for your consideration. I look forward to meeting with you.

—Olivia

About a week before the meeting James received her agenda for prior perusal and acknowledged receipt. Further, he sent her a reply saying he would expect her on the agreed date and at the appointed time.

It took tremendous courage for Olivia to address the incidents and their issues from a values mind-set, but when she did so, she and James were able to talk civilly and constructively based on the mutual benefits of the goals they both shared. This discussion led Olivia to ask James for permission to address how the general working environment could improve; he agreed to consider this with her. As part of her plan, she positioned the benefits of top and managerial leadership's unity that should be evidenced in their presence, along with increased affirmation, renewed commitment to organizational health, and departmental and personnel successes.

James respected her leadership, and told her so. She granted him respect in return. This was surely a gift he had not earned from his position alone, but one she had granted to him for the greater benefit of all.

The immediate result was that she was heard and given permission to implement many of her plans of engagement in company production improvement and leadership development. After all, they weren't going to cost much. It was during the implementation of one of Olivia's plans that James was introduced to the three leadership tracks, and saw how his leadership in many respects could improve, if he so chose. The resulting journeys upon which Olivia embarked, to walk James and two other senior VP's through the tracks (at his request), also became the impetus for her to take leadership training to two other employees accountable to her that had requested the same input, along with two other managers.

The finished products of these investments are still in development. The internal work environment has changed as employees cooperate to form a shared value system; behaviors are willfully starting to come in line with expressed desires for improvement based on newly established core values. People are declaring what they want without fear of recrimination, as opposed to expressing what they don't want in an atmosphere of intimidation. Solutions are coming from freedom to state a problem within the understanding that for every problem presented, one or two solutions must be positioned as well for consideration. Staffers are showing through their actions they are committed to achieving an improved work culture and greater and more accurate production through vastly improved communication and trust. A recipe is developing for achieving success in growing people and function simultaneously. While this continues to be an uphill path in some respects because people change slowly, the process is working and proving the worth of the efforts.

Leadership confronts difficult situations with truth, thoughtfully presented and timely placed, inclusive of clearly articulated and verifiable goals stemming from a desire to fulfill a cause greater than the discomfort of the moment, and in anticipation of greater wins at the end.

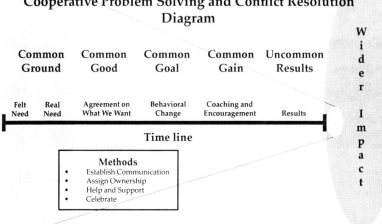

Cooperative Problem Solving and Conflict Resolution Diagram

You, as the investment leader, will take the initiative when you see that a value system needs to be constructed. You will choose well if you decide to engage the follower in the process of its creation. You, as the leader, will point the way to incorporating certain immutable standards that are vital parts of the constitution of the system.

A value system is founded on standards shown to be time tested and therefore able to be trusted because they are true and enduring. A leader with a long-term legacy-focused view reflects on a value system's degrees of solidarity, or sticking power, whether or not they have stood the tests of agelessness, and still hold true in current activity. Evidences of what is "right" become proofs that can be repeated in daily experiences.

Evidences of the Staying Power of a Value System

Listed below are some of the most important evidences of the staying power of a value system. They should not be viewed in isolation; grouped together they form a continuum of certainty; when these are working together, they help complete the person and the process.

Internal Fulfillment

When a decision about what is valued is connected to high moral principles, the choice maker is encompassed with an internal sense that he or she is making right and good decisions in the development of a value system. Internal guides, senses of right and wrong, or conscience as some would call it, tells the truth to those who would listen and possess a capacity and desire to heed what the internal voice is saying. The "rule of law" founded on guiding principles that for millennia has pointed out correct paths versus lawless ones gives added dimension to internal fulfillment. When what is chosen is proven right on the pattern of history's "yes" and good has resulted, people are benefited in condition and hope, and the inner voice affirms that choice.

External Contributions that Add Significance

A value system that contributes positive dimension to a person's existence and a group's product has to be measured according to its degree of worth in external application.

When right choices are made, action-results prove their rightness. External contributions that lift condition and cause gratification follow. In short, production validates choice.

An observer will see contributions in external real life applications that cause changes for the good. These consequences bolster confidence. In business, clearly observed results may include profitability along with the intentional building of people. In personal conduct, negative habits change into positive behaviors. These new behaviors agree with and contribute to the good of those who desire higher ethics and better standards. These affirmative external contributions raise the importance of a person's worth and encourage quality in what he or she produces. The bottom line: the evidences seen on the outside corroborate the right decisions made on the inside.

Objective Analysis

Objective analysis is more readily received when it comes from a person who the receiver knows really cares. Combining truth within care and compassion is a formula for success in analysis that when purposefully put into place never fails to achieve more benefit than cold truth declared in a relational vacuum.

Behavioral systems that would avoid or prevent relational connections, if they could even be termed as systems of "value," disallow impartiality because they are disconnected from the source that creates their very reason for existence: their desire for truth and the true means of expressing it. Objectivity never implies nor includes aloofness or relational separation; indeed the opposite is true. Objectivity sees the reality of a situation, and because it is born of trusting relationships it wants to tell the truth. Objectivity becomes possible and credible when the dread of getting too close is replaced by a desire to live without fear of failure or recrimination, and within the focus of the good that can result.

One who desires to create a value system welcomes objective analysis because it lives where applications of the principles live. Drawing back because of fear of being hurt is replaced by desire to be helped. Objectivity within a relationship opens the door to truth telling in an atmosphere of love. Love never hides from close observation; it embraces it. It not only has nothing to hide, it has its character to give away.

Proper Rewards

Value systems speak not only to what is good now, the standards that promote life; they also speak to fostering ongoing legacy, the benefits to succeeding generations. Value systems position character to last and endure.

Not giving in to sacrificing character on an altar of expediency will in time profit from this right choice. Upholding right character is its own reward and often elicits other worthwhile returns. A value system that promotes positive behavior will be a place where intangibles like trust and truth, honesty and faithfulness form the basis of good activity and gratification. If these intangibles are not present, they are certainly noticed by their absence; if they are present, they mold better ways of doing things, and they shape the rewards for beneficial behavior. A profit may or may not be evidenced as tangible in nature (more money, fame, "things"); regardless, profit honestly gained from good behaviors will always possess intangible merits.

Proper rewards for creating and living in a value system consistent with principle come in like manners born of the choices that first gave them life. Rewards for constructing and abiding in a value system of positive intangibles which against their existence no one can argue and against the validation of the proof of their contributions no reasonable person disputes, will come in like fashion as the character of their investments: where love is sown, love is reaped; where truth is planted, truth is harvested; where trust is extended, trust will be returned. As Emerson has explained, proper rewards, commensurate in scope and degree of likeness of character because they are based on the Laws of Sowing and Reaping, and Compensation will assuredly come in time. This promise is guaranteed, its system has repeated itself since memory began.

In the investment leadership track, constructing a value system upon which to build good and lasting legacy requires consideration of the character contributions all participants bring for consideration. Character matters most, and upon a mutual understanding of what constitutes good character, a value system can be constructed, form a basis for living, and become the source for prospering.

When the leader and follower combine the elements of their lists into a value system, they commit to believing with the head, espousing through the heart and employing with the hand. There is no distance between the attributes of character and the actions of choice. Results are like that too; there is no difference in the attributes of what is invested and what is obtained. There are no isolated theories and lottery-type hopes in these transactions; the value system creators are in charge of what they sow, and know for certain that in like manner, but in exponential amounts, their rewards will surely come.

Seven Life-Changing Questions

Posed here are seven life-changing questions a leader and follower with integrity should consider as they purpose to construct a core values list and their value system in which they will dwell. You are invited to weigh these carefully.

1. To what degree are you willing to show, and not just tell, desiring to demonstrate what you want as opposed to complaining about what you may not have? *This is a question to determine level of ownership at which a participant is willing to engage and what the reasonable expectations are.*

2. How willing are you to listen to and accept opinions

other than your own if these can be shown to make you a better person who will contribute out of developing strength? *This is a question that reveals the degree of willingness and desire for change when behavior is matched up against agreed values.*

3. How submissive are you at your core, and where does meekness (strength under proper control) fit into your concept of learning and leadership? *This question seeks to understand if humility is a choice for the participant, and if it is, where its effects are seen in the process of receiving instruction and setting examples of following and leading for others.*

4. How obedient are you in your manner, obeying in principle (attitudes that presage action) and in practice (habits that prove dedication)? *This question looks carefully at the desire for obedience to shared core values that will be seen in words of agreement, and behaviors that demonstrate the validity of those words.*

5. To what extent do you support and engage in division and sharing of responsibilities, especially behind the scenes? *This question looks at how much weight a participant gives to taking credit and needing applause, whether or not longing to be at a center of acknowledgment becomes so important as to form the birthplace for arrogance and aggrandizement.*

6. What is the fulfillment you receive from willingly servicing others? *This question measures the degree of*

cooperation and shows to what extent the participant wants to put others first, supporting, encouraging, and giving to them.

7. How committed are you to achieving the mutual benefits produced when improved behavior and more excellent provision are the results of collective devotion to higher standards of people-development on the part of each team member? *This question views the commitment level to building relationships: making decisions to support another's success, and their corroborating function, the actions that validate the truth of those decisions, and whether when one participant achieves, the results are truly celebrated without jealousy, rather, with joy; and to what degree if any the participant desires credit for his or her contribution.*

A Value System and the Effectiveness Proofs

The formation of a value system where right principles are positioned to produce right practices must be measured against standards that endure. That a list of principled concepts are termed "standards" becomes its own indicator that these attributes of character withstand and have withstood not only tests of time, but the examination of highest qualities that right-standing people embrace. These standards are and have been consistently repeated within lives and works of moral people throughout the millennia whose lives are exemplary.

Whenever these kinds of standards are applied to living, they cause behaviors to change for the better and the quality of life to improve. These standards encourage people of truth to willfully align themselves with what has been shown to work within all natural settings and social environments: culture to culture, continent to continent, and age to age.

A value system in formation must be weighed against standards of proven results. Standards qualify as pillars of character-resilience because they cannot be altered if they are true; none more resilient to human existence will have ever been nor will ever need to be created if the modeled standards are shown to be right and trustworthy. Therefore, a list of standards should not need to be reinvented; indeed, a true list has been around for a very long time.

An investment leader and follower who become engaged in development of a value system as part of their run on the investment leadership track will compare their list of values with a list of solid standards to see if and how their list measures up. The more agreement exists between the enduring standards and their list of core values, the greater the strength of the value system they design and to which they agree to abide.

The list below consists of living standards and these are brought to life and bring life every time they are employed. Indeed they live whether they are employed or not. Your job as the leader is to activate them for you and the people you lead.

These standards constitute nine "proofs" of resiliency and dependability for anyone who wishes to engage in their effectiveness by living out the principled values they produce. They are both tools that can be used to create a value system and the measurement grid of that system's worth. Further, these standards, these indelible proofs, are available to and achievable by anyone at any time. Their use will always alter life. They are "proofs" because, simply put, they've endured in their attestation, and permanently will.

Investment leaders are certain beyond all doubt that to the degree they align themselves and the processes they employ on behalf of their followers to the values that originate with, and produce these proofs, the more unyielding assurances exist that the investments they seek to make will endure for the right reasons, producing results of legacy that will be seen in selfless-serving, other's-benefit ensuing, positive outcomes for as long as they are employed. They reproduce themselves and change every life they touch.

If you are the leader, adapt these, and your legacy will live.

Nine Proofs of a Value System's Validity and Endurance*

1. Love: a decision of the will, evidenced in a commitment and corroborating action to make a positive difference in another's life, regardless of the cost.
2. Joy, or happiness: not necessarily its pursuit, rather, the fulfillment within the processes of seeing and

helping another person succeed, where the decisions and engagements that constitute the process are more important than the product and the means because its quality gives birth and credence to its end.

3. Satisfaction, or dwelling in peace: an inner state of involved contentment that originates from acts of doing right things, simply because they are the right things to do, where others are benefited, whether or not they are aware of their benefactors.

4. Patience: a decision to extend forbearance and timely understanding to others and one's self on a journey of personal development that is often punctuated with pain and problems to overcome.

5. Kindness: deliberate actions toward others that prove to be beneficial to them, caring more about another person's gain than what may or may not come as a reward to the person who generates the good deeds.

6. Goodness: seen or unseen expressions of virtue, morality, and unselfishness, participating in higher standards of ethical activity that elevate others' conditions or places.

7. Faithfulness: the overt evidence of dedication and follow-through seen in consistent obedience to proper authority; where, regardless of circumstances, levels of comfort, perceived or real expectations, or personal cost, a commitment is upheld and fulfilled, period.

8. Gentleness: handling other people's persons,

personalities, emotions, welfare, existence and presence with care, consideration, dignity and compassion.

9. Self-control: the desire, decision and cultivated ability to exercise meekness (strength that is utilized by degrees within willful and personally designed confines of correct positioning for greatest and most beneficial results), placing one's self in subjection to lawful order, and the resilience to repeat the behaviors that demonstrate this attribute regardless of time, circumstance, convenience or lack thereof, comfort level, and perceived or real outcomes.

*Ancient Jewish Stoicism literature quoted and adapted by Paul the Apostle (formerly Saul of Tarsus), in Galatians 5:22, 23 of the *Holy Bible* (NIV)

These nine proofs become "The Standards" against which all value systems are measured in terms of origin, application and effectiveness. Where any value system results in all nine proofs in actual experience, that value system can be stated to be "certain" as regards to good character quality, is devoid of inherent defects, and possesses seeds of regenerative longevity in design, nature and projected outcomes, regardless of forms, languages, expressions or means of delivery.

Any value system that does not produce these proofs in whole combination does not constitute a system of meritorious character in its core makeup and should be discarded all together, or reconstructed and realigned to the proofs that stand.

You, as an investor leader, if the investment track is your track of choice, and if you want to build enduring legacy, will see that the constitution of your value system will stand the test of and beyond your time, because it is proven by the standards that have done so. You will remember that the value system erected on these standards uses them as tools for its construction as well as measuring devices of its success, at the same time.

Your job as the leader is to consistently evaluate your behaviors and those of your follower alongside your value system, and your value system next to the nine proofs. You will persevere toward the goal of total concert of relationship and function, demonstrated in whole and in part, and you will encourage your follower to emulate your devotion to this end, because you are building your legacy. Will you do it?

This is an awesome and rewarding responsibility, but one a leader in the investment leadership track welcomes.

Mentoring for Life Change

Integrating a proven value system into life application is best accomplished through a process called mentoring. The investment track leader understands and uses mentoring as a valued procedure.

Mentoring is both a condition and an action, where

investments from leader to follower occur through the creation of transferable models of relational strength and functional accountability, in a predetermined time frame with predetermined goals by which to measure degrees of success. Mentoring is best achieved when the one who would mentor is being mentored, and has experienced the benefits of the mentoring process.

Developing a mentoring relationship takes diligence in desire, spending precious time and other resources to find the people and engage them, assuring that both the mentor and the one to be mentored understand the relationship and all its factors.

Mentoring Factors

An investment leader knows the high importance of this endeavor, sees it as essential and determinable, and runs on this track in full understanding of its *parameters*. Not content with a theory of how mentoring should look, mentoring participants choose and agree on specific actions within which behavioral change is defined and expected and therefore able to be measured as to its success or missing the mark.

To begin the mentoring *process*, to mentor or to be mentored:

1. **Find a mentor and become a mentor**. This endeavor calls for *perseverance*, sometimes more than one

anticipates. Settle only for a mentoring relationship that has the best chances for success and take the time to build it well.

2. **Look for a right mentor "match."** Participants' agreements align on their reason for this relationship. This match is the foundation of their *plan* to assure its success.

3. **Become a student, remain a learner.** Both mentor and mentored must show continuing *proof* of willingness to receive instruction.

4. **Be accountable and faithful in a current position, whether constructive or adverse, until you have finished well.** Growing out of one station and into another does not usually mean the abandonment of the first. Rather, the *pursuit* of growth means that the mentor or the one being mentored works through current difficulties to learn the lessons of growth the stages may include and only moves on when a proper replacement has been found and thoroughly trained.

5. **Desire to grow.** Earnest longing for maturity, seen in acquiring knowledge and applying wisdom is a *prerequisite* for the mentor and mentored who desire to eventually see the results coming from their declared desires.

6. **Seek to associate with people who either "are where I want to be" or who aspire to develop leadership skills "similar to what I want."** Models are transferable and

often interchangeable, associations with *people* who have built good models are desirable and should be pursued.

7. **Ask questions.** Posing thoughtful questions is a communication art vital to the mentoring arrangement. It deliberately locates the one who wants to learn in the best *place* to receive instruction.

8. **Listen to answers.** Answers to interrogatories stand disconnected unless they are wholeheartedly received. To be received, they have to be heard; intentional listening becomes part of a participant's *performance* in mentoring.

9. **Read and become intellectually acquainted with ideas that stretch and challenge your mind.** Information sources are boundless. Mentor arrangements intently seek *positions* to gain education that broaden and expand levels of knowledge. Mentoring relationships never impose limits on learning.

10. **Apply learning.** When learning is applied its *presence* is seen in actual life. Those who learn are responsible for owning the outcomes of their own application, and show how the lessons are shaping living, because it is shaping them.

11. **Seek truth and live within it.** Never settling for less than a full measure of devotion, a mentoring arrangement conforms to its defined and designed *purpose*: a commitment to truth in content and context.

12. **Share core values in actions dedicated to building up, not tearing down.** *Principles* engaged in real life change it, and when anchored to values, seek the best for all those they touch.

13. **Earnestly desire to live in an understanding of a values-focused framework.** Ideals that become life-decisions showcase their *perspective*, no matter the odds. People engaged in mentoring procedures openly share their viewpoints to see if they stand up to scrutiny.

14. **Continue to seek and listen to older, wiser and maturing models from whom to obtain information and counsel.** This is a *pollination* of life-wisdom that benefits both mentor and the one being mentored. There is always someone who knows more, is wiser, and has encouragement to give. Mentoring says: find them, hear them, and put the values of their contributions into your life.

15. **Hunger for investment and to invest.** Insatiable longing for opportunities to build into and receive from others constitutes an enduring *paradigm* that doesn't shift. It is not moved by circumstances, whims, or temporary fads. It is built on a value system and nine proofs and builds legacy.

The Engagement of Mentoring

Mentoring may be best described as "life-upon-life"

investment. Highly engaged, it is never detached from its object or accomplished at a distance. It's close, upfront and very personal and the degree of proximity between investment leader and follower matters greatly.

Mentoring begins when a mentor and one who would be mentored agree to an engagement and cooperatively design the program they will follow. In their design, they will build from the Code of Achievement, ask the Four Questions, create their value system, and inquire: What are my greatest celebrations and challenges and what do I need to learn through them? Will you work with me to discover the answers to these questions, and show me how to apply them to my life?

Mentoring is instructional, disseminates information and requires learning. This instruction is in a form of give and take: it is hands-on, discussion-engaged, and activity-oriented.

Mentoring is a time-line-sensitive process. While learning is life-long, mentoring, to be most effective, has a specified beginning and a specified end. Its duration is generally months, not weeks or years.

Mentoring is highly achievement-focused, with definitions of wins clearly understood from the outset. Within its time frame, reasonable expectations are described and agreed upon, evaluated, corrected, and celebrated. Mentoring provides the structure and focus that help the participants reach their goals.

Mentoring requires consistency and is not content with off again and on again interactions; in fact, it abhors them. Consistency of the process is seen in dedication to defining and finishing details, calendaring "To Do" items and requiring they are fulfilled. Absence of one negatively affects all.

Mentoring is motivational; it encourages people to become all it is possible for them to become and to accomplish all they are capable of accomplishing. Nurture, support and encouragement are distributed and used in abundance. The applause is long and freely given as the mentored moves from success to success.

Mentoring is emotionally rewarding to investment leader and follower; joy comes more from the process than the product; celebrations and just plain fun punctuate a successful mentoring relationship. People engaged in mentoring processes don't take themselves too seriously, even though the process is serious. A maturing person will laugh at him or herself, and engage in humor along the way.

Mentoring for life-change creates disciplined people who obey established core values because they agree on their constitution and applicability, and because they agree that their obedience to those values becomes proof positive of their dedication to this life-giving relationship and the future it promises.

Leadership investors want investments that pay back—in exponential return. Creating a model of leadership that works is hard work. Running on the track of investment leadership demands a tremendous expenditure of energy. But when the baton is passed, when the decision has been made to finish well, a proven value system has been reproduced into real experience, and in the mentoring process the follower and leader accomplish great strides. They have created and are living within a model of leadership investment that is, in fact, working.

This is What Leadership Is—
Chapter 7:
Creating Leadership Models that Work

Review and Reinforce:

1. A "model" is a living entity who, in character and condition, illustrates the cause and actualization of relationships; where participants willingly decide and adopt principles and corroborating actions in environments they create, that foster consistency, thrive on integrity, earnestly seek excellence, and duplicate their effectiveness over time by investing in others of like passion, so that the product of the original is greater than the original itself.
2. In the creation of the model and those that would emulate it, the future is assured and the baton is passed.
3. Finish well.
4. Construct a value system.
5. The "Twelve Laws of Understanding" can serve as an illustration of a value system.
6. Base your value system on nine proofs, standards that have withstood the test of time.
7. Integrating a proven value system into life is best accomplished through mentoring.
8. Not content with a theory of how mentoring should

look, mentoring participants choose and agree on specific actions within which behavioral change is defined and expected and therefore able to be measured as to its success or missing the mark.

9. Mentoring may be best described as "life-upon-life" investment.

10. Mentoring for life-change creates disciplined people who obey established core values because they agree on their constitution and applicability, and because they agree that their obedience to those values becomes proof positive of their dedication to this life-giving relationship and the future it promises.

8
Moving People

Leaders running in impact, influence and investment leadership tracks all seek opportunities to move people into greater arenas of maturity. They want to promote progression from an impact track to an influence track to the investment track, if in fact their followers want to be moved. They want to see growth of relationships with followers mature from dependence through independence into inter-dependence.

Movement is directly related to motive, and where the leader and follower share the same motives, anchored in their mutual agreements in a code of achievement and a proven value system, then progress toward maturity is likely ready to occur.

Moving people requires cooperation that comes from the strength of resilient relationships: both parties making quality decisions about supporting one another's success, and in the leader's case, freely supplying the tools a follower needs to help establish his or her own success. A leader's initiative encourages a follower's movement toward growth, with that follower's permission. Bottom line: if you are the leader, you need to determine if your follower wants to move, and if the answer is "yes," then mentor them accordingly.

Open-ended Questions

One of the clearest and cleanest ways for a leader to determine if a follower is ready to move forward toward greater maturity is to ask. Using open-ended questions that cannot be answered with a simple "yes" or "no" is generally preferable. Samples of questions a leader might ask of the follower could include:

1. What kind of progress do you think we could make together if we sought a more focused leadership investment for you?

2. How willing would you be to engage in additional and progressive steps of growth that it appears you may be ready to take?

3. If it could be shown that you were prepared for more responsibility and greater degrees of leadership impact or influence, how open would you be to this possibility?

4. Progress is often achieved when people are stretched; at what point would you be willing to be stretched more, to grow in your impact or influence?

Listening to the answers questions like these produce is vital. The techniques of engaged listening, as have been referenced previously, are part of the art of communication. These may include repeating answers back to assure clarity, perhaps using alternate but accurate words to assure understanding, and pinpointing specific actions for the follower and leader to take, that if completed will conclusively prove that real communication is occurring.

If you are the leader, ask and listen properly. You will more likely pick up true answers if you provide the full amount of time the follower needs to answer truly, so avoid rushing or pushing. Don't interrupt. Instead, showing genuine courtesy, reposition a question or the timing of its presentation if you need to, to allow the follower to think and engage at a deeper level. Spend the time and energy, but spend it with decorum that promotes dignity and encourages participation.

Consider the title of this Chapter: "Moving People." The word "moving" can be a verb or an adjective, depending on the meaning desired. Place it as a verb first and adjective second in this next sentence, and see if a concept rings true: Moving people is accomplished only through moving people. In other words, moving (verb) people is only possible when the leader can be described as already in motion, and the follower wants to match his or her stride. It is hard if not impossible for a leader to encourage movement if the leader is immobile.

A follower who is reticent, or a leader who is too busy or not interested, by their attitudes and actions will declare, "I shall not be moved!" and indeed they won't if their minds are set on remaining stationary. If you are the leader who wants to move and your follower doesn't, simply deal with that follower within the track he or she has chosen, and look for someone else to receive your investment leadership efforts. If you are the leader who doesn't want to move yourself, consider that the development of your living legacy is on hold.

When presented with the option of progressing to another track, a follower with bigger dreams, regardless of the track in which the leader is running, will probably be itching to consider advancement, if not visibly enthusiastic about the whole process. Some virtually explode with excitement at the prospect. Others, when presented with options of forward movement, show the "deer in the headlights" glare of pure, unadulterated fear. This indication says to the leader, "Slow down the process!" It may even mean the leader with the follower agree to temporarily or permanently shelve it.

Moving people against their will is a foolish waste of resources. Don't even try. Too many leaders waste too much time in endeavoring to inculcate desire that is not present within the make-up of a follower. Believe it, because it's true: the follower who wants to grow will let the leader know.

The follower who wants to grow will let the leader know.

Investor leaders look for people who are motivated and desire movement. Investor leaders are willing to run the track of discovery for the benefit of the person who wishes to be mentored, and are willing to pay the prices necessary for this follower to become the best he or she can become, if that follower, with integrity, demonstrates earnest desire for that investment.

Followers who want or don't want to move tell their leader in many ways. The communications of "yes" or "no" come from attitudes, body language, words, deeds, follow-through or lack of it…. You get the idea.

Because followers tell a leader whether or not they want to be part of the leader's structure of investment and mentoring, a leader's job is to read the signs, listen to the words, study the interactions, pay close attention and respond with integrity to the totality of communications the follower is sharing. One of the great faults of leaders who are not aware is that they miss these signals. A maturing leader regularly scans for them. Movement that matters is only possible when the yearning is present. If you are a leader, look intently and intentionally for what a follower is showing you, watch the signals, listen to the conversations, and observe the actions. All will point to a true degree of desire, or its desultory absence.

In an investing relationship where a follower jumps at the prospect of growth and takes ownership to begin it, a leader/mentor is in the best position to help that person move. Creating action steps to initiate and implement this movement is part of preparing to pass the baton, and is a task filled with anticipation that is shared by both investor-leader and receiver-follower.

If you are the leader, you will see that it is simply amazing and incredibly fulfilling to watch the progress while you share in the parts you play. Participation and progress, and movement to fulfill mission—these fit each other like a hand in a glove. There is great satisfaction when all occur together.

Tools

Many tools are available to promote movement in people development. Some tools are more profitable than others. Moving people requires knowledge of these tools, the wisdom to choose the right ones, and the training to utilize them in correct ways. The leader takes the initiative to determine the tools and their use. As with other choices included in *Leadership Is—*, the responsibility of accurate and best choices of which tools to use and how they are applied belongs to the leader.

The tools are varied in style and scope, and their applications set up wins or losses. Right tools and applications frame potential for great relational and functional results; wrong tools with their misapplications can be incredibly damaging to both relationships and functions, for both leader and follower.

Four tools are considered here. Two are recommended, and two are to be rejected. All four are defined and discussed in detail. A wise leader will consider these tools, and based on the merits and not necessarily the popularity, choose for impact, influence and investment. The results of the choices of tools will be seen almost immediately upon their initial application.

Motivation

Motivation is a strong and recommended tool a leader employs to initiate progression for a follower, to see if that follower desires what a leadership investment can create.

Motivation is not hype; it is help that a leader gives a follower to see processes and related results as a unified whole. Motivation is a process in which the leader describes an engagement and consequences, and stimulates desires for action on the basis of what is portrayed. A leader motivates when the future is described realistically, and the follower responds optimistically because he or she wants it and will work for it.

Proper motivation transfers the ownership of desire and willingness to work, into the action and life-experience of the follower. A temptation for the leader is to try to move a follower too quickly, or motivate without establishing ownership on the part of the follower. When this occurs, the efforts will have come from and therefore will remain with the leader. The follower is not wholly participating because he or she can't, or won't. While a leader's desire to see a follower succeed may originate from a pure motive, the leader must assure that the methods of motivation are so engaged within the follower's desires that eventually they flow from the follower.

Transfer of Ownership

Transfer of ownership occurs when motivation is working; in fact, these two aspects of movement are uniquely tied together. The signs that the transfer from leader to follower is taking place are these:

- Yearning on the part of the follower to fulfill obligations without having to be pushed
- Follower's completion of tasks with excellence, and ahead of time
- Follower's attention to detail, exercising faithfulness
- Follower trying innovation, coming up with ideas on his or her own
- Follower willfully assuming tasks that others may not want
- Follower asking for more opportunities
- Follower taking initiative: prior to bringing problems forward to discussion, follower has proactively created solutions and presents the problems only with the solutions accompanying them
- Follower proactively reporting on status of tasks or completion of responsibilities before the leader even asks

- Follower reaching and teaching other people within an impact or influence track because the follower desires to impart what he or she is learning
- Follower reporting progress to people other than the leader, expanding the network
- Follower asking thoughtful questions and acting on answers
- Follower desiring to learn from additional sources and share that learning with leader and others

The leader's responsibility is to acquaint the follower with these signs of transfer of ownership and teach their processes to the learner. If you are the leader, make sure you communicate them well and celebrate whenever they are seen in action.

Further, the leader's expectation is that the follower who really wants the investment to pay off will be attuned to the signs within him or herself, and stimulate further engagement when the transfers start to occur; in other words, ask and reach for more.

Motivation recognizes and promotes the need for excellence. A true examination of satisfaction looks at the standard in a current line of excellence, observing whether it meets or exceeds expectations. A leader engaged in motivation will ask, "When will your current line of excellence become your new line of mediocrity? When will your desires to do better set new levels toward which you will strive?" Leaders want followers to set their own lines of achievement, surpass them, and set new levels to attain. Investment leaders eagerly promote these measures.

Motivation comes from the leader's desire to see the student or follower succeed in a healthy balance of relationship and function; and the leader talks of this openly and encourages it often. One of the ways to assure that your leadership motivation is pure and working properly is to evaluate it this way: "Are the relationships (decisions based on shared core values) and functions (actions that validate decisions) in balance? Is character being strengthened and are commitments of excellence in productivity observable?"

Listen to the answers to those questions.

Motivation seeks to identify a real need and fill it. While motivation cares and responds to felt need as a viable entry point in dealing with incidents, it refuses to dwell there; rather, it instigates investigation to discover real needs, focuses on issues beneath the surface and then satisfies them with resolutions that work.

The establishment of motivation originates from the code of achievement. A value system weighs its progression.

Motivation thrives on variety in accomplishing its goals. The means of motivation are purposefully integrated holistically with the ends, and diversity of application is endorsed.

Motivation is concerned with helping people improve through the growth of their relationships to empower them to accomplish more in their functions, with qualified excellence.

Motivation is heartily recommended, and if you are the development leader, you will more likely assure integral and integrity-filled success into your follower's experience and the creation of your legacy when this tool as described is employed in the investment and mentoring processes.

Manipulation

Opposite of motivation is manipulation, a process characterized by a focus centered at the end of the day upon the leader's welfare. Manipulation is often seen as getting the follower to do what the leader wants done, to fulfill a leader's desires and demands, but not necessarily for the good of the follower. Investment leadership does not manipulate; indeed it rejects this tool because at its core it violates the principle that people are more important than what they do.

Manipulation connives to position activity for the purpose of achievement in isolation of relationship building or character enhancement. Manipulation illustrates a desire to elevate performance over personal worth and is willing to eliminate a relationship if the performance is more valuable to the task's completion at that time, or any time. Manipulation is utilitarian in nature: the follower is only as good as what the follower can produce.

Manipulation more readily assumes a need, positioning the leader's perceptions of what the needs are, above the follower's. In this way, the leader listens rarely, or if at all, ineffectually; enters discussions with prior intentions decided; and leaves little room for dialogue, interaction, or discovery.

Manipulation seeks to push people through a template, or prescriptive "one size fits all" means of accomplishing goals. Without engaging in due diligence, the end often justifies the means. Directives become more important than discussion. Without pursuing constructive communication, conversation is often avoided all together.

Manipulation does not stand the test of a comparison to a truth-based value system or the endurance of a vision whose primary focus is building people first. Nor does manipulation cooperate with instilling a message of hope, nor fulfillment of a mission of making a difference. Instead, through a violation of basic principles, it prods people to produce more whether they become better or not and ignores personal worth in the face of "getting the job done," settling for quantity of product instead of quality of person.

A leader who agrees with the *Leadership Is—* way of thinking and acting will not use manipulation.

Deputizing

The selection of this word is intentional. A deputy, as *Leadership Is—* defines the term, is a follower who acts with the absolute authority and within the commensurate responsibility of the one who deputized him or her. In full faith, demonstrated character, observable attitudes and resolute action, the deputy is a competent and therefore complete representative of the originator. When the deputy speaks, the leader speaks, and when the deputy acts, it is with the prior and whole agreement of the leader, on his or her behalf, and usually at the leader's behest.

An investment leader who seeks to deputize a follower, and establish that follower as a trustworthy component of the leader's authority, helps the follower recognize his or her inherent worth, and gives that follower all the understanding needed, to know beyond any doubt what a right course of action is, or the processes to determine it. The follower-turned-deputy sees the leader exercise these dedicated and deliberate actions toward empowering that deputy, and responds with actions that fulfill his or her responsibilities well. A deputy wants to achieve what is requested and required of this new position, and sets about doing it with confidence, authority, and responsibility.

Deputizing creates a reproducible model of the code of achievement to encourage positive attitudes and produce right actions in completion of organizational or investment goals. Following the code of achievement prepares leader and follower for the passing of the baton.

Deputizing builds responsibility through leadership's exercise of accountability to the follower. Through example, the leader demonstrates the how and why of accomplishing assigned tasks well, an example of following authority. Remember, the requirement of the leader is to teach the follower how to follow before the leader teaches the follower how to lead. Deputizing showcases this investment process well.

Deputizing is an unmistakable and highly disciplined decision to mentor through investing. In its process of development, deputizing asks for and obtains proper permission from the follower for the follower to grow, stretch, and learn in the context of a maturing relationship.

Deputizing is possible because a follower has a goal: to look and act like the leader. The leader removes obstacles to this goal and imparts every encouragement and assistance to more than fulfill it, commending the deputy to achieve even more than the one who deputizes.

Deputizing teaches proactively, not passively, and encourages obedience to shared values through integrating those values into actions of daily living.

Deputizing shows its effectiveness in exemplary modeling so that when the follower leads, the leader's authority is clearly seen.

Deputizing builds upon the strengths of the leader and follower by considering each individual's abilities, essentials of their composite natures, their seasons of life; deputizing seeks to create responsibilities to fit ability and capability, and celebrates its wins.

Deputizing includes intentional listening, confronts error with truth and satisfies relational vacuums with appropriate care.

Deputizing is heartily recommended.

While motivation promotes movement, deputizing authorizes success. If you are an investment leader, you will deputize your most-likely-to-succeed candidates based on properly qualifying and nurturing them through quality investments to help assure their correct and balanced contributions, especially when you are not present.

Deputizing as an investment tool to move people is utilized fully when the one who is deputized becomes the originator of the process all over again into a follower of his or her own. This duplicative model is fulfilled when the baton is passed within the investment leadership track. Legacy is the result.

Delegating

Leadership Is— does not prefer delegating, in fact, it condemns this term because as it is tied to tasks within business environments, it usually indicates the opposite of what constitutes deputizing and is not contributory to business and life investment models.

Delegating often ignores people building, preferring function alone, and in that regard as a process it may promote the completion of a job, but it does not reach toward relationships, nor teach life lessons that last beyond a job's completion.

As this book defines delegating, it is a process of task-passing that may or may not include relational foundations or caring influence. It is focused mainly on duty fulfillment, whether or not personal growth of the one to whom an assignment is delegated is allowed or encouraged to occur.

Investment leadership rejects delegating within this definition because, like manipulation, it violates the central premise of: people are more important than what they do, and relationships precede and give definition to function.

Delegation may conclude that the one who delegates still owns ultimate responsibility, but this facet of the delegation process is rarely communicated and understood, or taken to heart if articulated. When delegated tasks are assigned, the process may allow failures, if they occur, to be forgotten and foster gross lack of accountability where no one takes responsibility. Where success is not realized from an assignment, delegation can fuel the fires of blame with the gasoline of guilt, building cases against employees who fail in their efforts. Fault-finding and finger pointing reign. Delegation can also create an environment of task-only focus where people are valued only for the assignments they're given, and only if they fulfill them.

Delegation is interested in job-action almost exclusively and pushes "doing" often without needed corresponding accountability or accompanying authority, presenting demands that a person perform, isolated from responsible relationships.

Delegation is interested in getting people to produce more than it considers potential personal cost or damage to a relationship an action could entail, especially if the product is one that requires a sacrifice the leader is not prepared to make.

Delegation assumes permission because of the leader's position, is communicatively weak, and may ask for forgiveness later if things go wrong. Followers are prone to wonder if recrimination will accompany any refusal to obey an order that is clearly not appropriate. Fear moves the follower to action, instead of confident assurance that a deed is right.

Delegation dictates assignments, rarely considering alternatives, and may not be open to suggestions or innovation.

Delegation identifies positional needs first and finds people to fill them often, whether or not the function and the person are a match. If the match is not present, the stress created when the person fails becomes the breeding ground for ongoing fault and discrediting. Should success be achieved, the person's value is only tied to the win. Integrity suffers here either way, and personal worth if it existed at all, is adversely affected.

Delegation may abide a lack of ethics or honesty if in the leader's perspective the end justifies the means. Leaders who delegate who are not centered in values, have been known to ask delegates to commit wrongdoing, and in doing so completely violate the principles of truth telling behind all that *Leadership Is*— represents. These principles say unequivocally that no one is required to break the law, or deny their ethics for the sake of fulfilling a delegated task.

Relationships in a framework of delegation are generally only as prominent as the procedures needed to wrap up an assignment; the value of the person is valuable only until the job is finished.

You are the investment leader, running in the investment leadership track, seeking to build your legacy. When you avoid delegation and manipulation, you become a modeling mentor. When you replace these two too-often misapplied tools with the far better tools of deputizing and motivation, you are providing greater leadership.

Investment track leadership lives for more than today's accomplishments. When confronted with options to choose expediency or compromise character, it avoids the urge to delegate and manipulate. Investment track leadership believes that people, rather than tasks, are the central concentration and uses motivation and deputizing to move people to greater levels of accomplishment, holding fast to values that will not change. Leadership intent on building legacy through people enjoys the prospects that every task and proper tool present as it fashions opportunities to pass the baton.

You are invited to build your people through your process because they are more important than what they do. Use motivation and deputizing to move them.

Living Proof: "Robert and His Warehouse"

Robert "owned" the warehouse, in the best sense of the word. Whenever most of the staff of fifty-seven needed to go there, they enjoyed dealing with Robert, affectionately known as "Bobber," because he was quite a fisherman, or so he said. At least he prided himself in the four antique fishing poles prominently displayed in his warehouse office. Quite a character, Bobber: his girth contributed to his gregarious nature (he had been a university football lineman of repute, had the trophies to show for it, and after ten years off the field still could fill a place), and his contagious smile consumed the entire lower half of his face. Normally, that grin was a fixture.

Bobber worked hard with his staff of thirteen warehouse-men, and these were divided into two groups for which he was responsible, one with five and a foreman, and one with six and its foreman. He had impact, and people respected him. He did his job well. During his five-year tenure, he had worked with many, had needed to fire very few, and was admired by the great majority of those who networked with him, simply because he was "there."

Bobber's boss, the VP of operations, had watched the camaraderie demonstrated in dealings with the warehouse, and for the most part was satisfied with product movement and timely response. Essentially their working relationship had been professionally distant; "You do your job; we don't need to talk." In spite of the VP's aloofness and avoidance of affirmation, there seemed to be a good balance of fun and production in Bobber's world.

But when that VP was replaced with Ken, things quickly began to change. The line of excellence enjoyed by Bobber and his teams quickly morphed into a line of mediocrity that had to be dealt with. The reality: Ken was a firm believer in progression, not status quo, and heartily agreed with and practiced leadership advancement, looking for rising stars to follow his example.

Within one week of Ken's arrival, a meeting occurred where Ken introduced Bobber to three tracks of leadership. Not only was Bobber greeted with an opportunity to choose an expanded leadership paradigm for his warehousemen who wanted to excel; Ken was asking Bobber if Ken could mentor him! No one in business or football had ever approached Bobber that way before.

Not unacquainted with challenges to conquer new goals, Bobber contemplated why he had settled on his current game stats, why he was internally resistant to creating new leadership opportunities for himself and his crews. He was making a comfortable living for himself and his family of three, and thought "moving up" was not really necessary. In fact, complacency had set in; he was content to get the job done and let his larger-than-life personality carry him. People in his purview had on occasion asked him for help on a surface, business level, and he was happy to give it most of the time. But if anyone got too close, wanted more than shipping and receiving technique and bills of lading information, he resisted. Folks who saw the smile but felt the separation excused the walls because they liked him and didn't want to offend.

Through Ken's invitation and investment, Bobber came to see that altering leadership's focus might or might not mean gaining position; this wasn't a matter of moving up; rather, "moving out" to expanded and inclusive leadership opportunities, both to give and receive. This was not about defending a line, or lining up boxes; this was about becoming an investor leader to the warehousemen who may want to grow through Bobber's model. Promotions, if they came, would be welcomed, but those were not the goal; building his people through being built himself was his new incentive.

Talk about change: over a six-month time frame, Bobber embarked on the journey with determination and chronicled both progress and setbacks in his journal. Within this process, he and Ken considered many reasons why Bobber, his team members, and the company would benefit when he chose perseverance. He realized that he was to seize new opportunities for growth daily. His smile didn't get any bigger, but his significance did.

In the short term, production increased. Executive staff noticed; and Bobber received invitations from two of his crew to invest in them, so he mentored them on "how to fish" in ways they hadn't previously considered. All because Ken taught Bobber some truth about motive and motivation, and Bobber listened and matured. In fact, one of Bobber's followers, Terry (formerly known by the name "Terror," wonder why?), became the new warehouse supervisor when the company's second warehouse location opened. Interestingly enough, it's a facility larger than the original, with twenty-one warehouse-men (and women) that look to Terry for leadership. Terry, of course, desires to run on all three leadership tracks, impacting and influencing while he looks for the next candidate for mentoring, as he himself once was.

Leadership that builds legacies is not content when a line of excellence becomes a line of mediocrity.

Treasures

People are valuable. They are a business's or group's most treasured resource, but often represent the most ineffectively used, squandered, or even discarded portion of a company's operational procedures when it bows to the urgency of a time line or the inconvenience of the moment.

Treated this way, it is no wonder that solid tools like motivation and deputizing are used as infrequently as they are; and akin to this observation, it is perfectly reasonable to conclude that manipulation and delegation are employed in their stead. Denying that people are more important than what they do promotes use of tools that wound; they are more quickly applied to meet the need of the moment, even though they are by their nature predisposed to disregard relational values of people who are not treasured, and are, rather, trashed.

In a business climate that demands immediate communication, uses people up, requires instant decisions and evaluates results faster than ever before, it is far easier to lose respect than to gain it, and far harder to take the time to build a relationship than to restrain it. But where a value system is created, vision articulated, mission understood and the message is permeated, the treasures become vital to a company's enduring success and are treated with the honor their value deserves. A time line for production may not be extended, but the template for evaluating the worth of the person is expanded. The inherent worth of the individuals and the respect their significance commands add more value to the treasured output these people provide.

There is no entitlement here; this is recognition of dignity. People are not robots; they're real, and should be treated realistically. Employees, followers of leaders in any of the three tracks, and students of investor teachers will be encouraged to grow when they are treated as treasures of investment; they will contribute value-added when bestowed proper value.

If you are the leader, it is to your and the company's best interests, in consideration of its core beliefs and bottom line, to build the work force, not force its work. Organizations that survive today will have better options to thrive tomorrow if they engage in building their people because they openly declare their merit. Merit produces meritorious service in people who want to grow, who understand that they are understood, are convinced they are vital to vitality, and know they can look to the employers not to be gold diggers, rather, to be investors in the treasures they are. This perspective builds promise, endures no matter the circumstances, and produces more value with the passing of time and the baton, in the building of a legacy.

Moving people is an objective and is possible when followers who are qualified are recipients of investments that come from a mentoring process of relationship building. Followers positioned for growth respond well to motivation and deputizing. An investment leadership based on the desire to move people for the right reasons will cause transferable growth on multiple levels: business, personal, within personnel and production. The goal of the leader, your goal if that's you, is to become so sensitized within your situation that none of this takes you by surprise. In fact, as you run in the investment track, you are energized because you are fully immersed in the deliberate planning and fulfillment of the whole leadership operation.

This is What Leadership Is—
Chapter 8:
Moving People

Review and Reinforce:

1. Leaders running in impact, influence and investment leadership tracks all seek opportunities to move people into greater arenas of maturity. They want to promote progression from an impact track to an influence track to the investment track, and from dependence through independence to relationships of inter-dependence, if in fact, their followers want to be moved.

2. Moving people requires cooperation that comes from the strength of resilient relationships.

3. If you are the leader, you need to determine if your follower wants to move, and if the answer is "yes," then mentor that follower accordingly.

4. Moving people is accomplished only through moving people. In other words, moving (verb) people is only possible when the leader can be described as already in motion, and the follower wants to match his or her stride.

5. Moving people against their will is a foolish waste of resources.

6. The follower who wants to grow will let the leader know.

7. Because followers tell a leader whether or not they want to be part of the leader's structure of investment and mentoring, a leader's job is to read the signs, listen to the words, study the interactions, pay close attention and respond with integrity to the totality of communications the follower is sharing.

8. Tools to use: motivation and deputizing.

9. Tools to reject: manipulation and delegating.

10. People are valuable. They are a business's or group's most treasured resource.

11. If you are the leader, it is to your and the company's best interests, in consideration of its core beliefs and bottom line, to build the work force, not force its work.

12. Moving people is an objective, and is possible when followers who are qualified are recipients of investments that come from a mentoring process of relationship building.

9
Leadership's Finish: Lines of Success

Leaders In Chapter 7, the differences between "finishing" and "finishing well" were described. You may want to review these definitions. The investment leadership track is a place where dreams and desires of legacies for the future are fashioned; it is also the place where finish lines of success are crossed, and the consummation of the investment brings about a living legacy and assures its future expansion. A living legacy is the proof of "finishing well."

Crossing finish lines of success will always include an exit. Business owners, entrepreneurs, and visionary leaders who have built enterprises begin at some point to look at leaving. They plan what their exiting should be and when it should start and often engage consultants to help them design strategies of egress. Goals in the process are to protect the business and promise its future thriving, as well as provide for the original leader as he or she moves on to another engagement. In building exit structures, insurance against loss is best accomplished by caring for and provisioning the people who are positioned best to carry on the enterprise and grow it once the initial or current leaders have departed.

Exit preparation doesn't pertain only to corporate executives, business owners, entrepreneurs, and visionaries, either. Exit preparation applies to every leader who occupies any position that will include the necessity at some point to leave it.

Planning for exit transitions is not easy, but is necessary. Preparation for exiting lays the groundwork for passing the baton. This passing marks the end of one investment and the beginning of another; the finalization of one developmental phase and the introduction of a new one. Exiting is required if the baton is to be passed. Running on the investment leadership track will always include exiting at some point, because the investment is time line sensitive. Also, an investment runner rarely runs in this track exclusively. An investment leader will be running on the impact and influence tracks at the same time. "Exiting" and "entering" time lines and activities on all three tracks may overlap and even intersect. A leader running in the investment track looks to pass the baton to his or her follower who is ready for this advancement, while simultaneously running on the impact and investment tracks to determine who may be ready for greater leadership investment when the opportunity comes.

Exiting and entering strategies for all tracks will include

the necessities the real world demands: legal requirements, financial considerations, executed agreements, full understandings, schedules, deadlines, completed tasks. Competence, experience, education, a résumé, references and past responsibilities count a great deal and loom large in consideration of a replacement of any leader. But "finishing well" exit strategies across the tracks should include more.

High on the list of placing people first and building investment leadership legacies that endure is the responsibility for the investor leader to learn which people out of any population are those the leader should consider for mentoring, who will have the greatest potential for the most enduring results, and who may qualify as replacements. The best successor may not be what a majority would consider the obvious "next in line" person, or the one with title-authority or the longest tenure. It could be a person with these credentials, but it also could not. Only a successful investment will tell.

An investment leader looks to pass his or her baton to the most qualified candidate. Finding and developing that candidate requires a leader's dedicated attention from a long-term point of view. Leaders will be energetically engaged in the processes of qualification and succession of the one who becomes the leader's replacement. This process will include intense observation, asking difficult questions, creating paths of integration—all parts of selecting the right person, place, time, responsibility, motive, and reward.

If you are the leader who is investing well and preparing

at some point to exit well, you consider proper exiting to be part of your desire to finish well. The expectations upon you are enormous and you need to fulfill the processes correctly.

When a successor is chosen, an investment leader will teach that successor to accomplish even greater works than the original leader has achieved. If you are the leader who desires legacy that lives beyond your presence, you will instantaneously comprehend that getting to a point of seeing "greater works" accomplished is tough, but because you know this is a good and right requirement of legacy, you will set the necessary parameters of greater production and will help your follower achieve them.

Transition Intersecting Points

A candidate to replace a leader brings relational and functional attributes that must be evaluated. These are matched with an organization's values, vision, mission and message to determine how many intersecting points exist.

These intersecting points are necessary to assure transitions born of agreement. Several of these points of desired intersection are listed here:

1. The need to match right person with right position
2. Levels of agreement with the Code of Achievement
3. Thoroughly investigating a candidate's internal values-based qualifications, using a tool like the Four Questions

4. Learning how much the candidate desires to enter an organization with a mandate to produce "greater works" than the leader who is leaving

5. How willing the current leader is to impart necessary tools, treasure, time and talent to help assure the success of the new leader

6. The due diligence required to discover functional capabilities: the candidate's levels of knowledge, understanding, education, experience and competence

7. The amounts of respect and trust remaining staff and leaders will freely grant to the new leader before the new leader earns them over time and experience

8. How much help remaining staff and leaders will contribute to assure a new leader's success

9. The degrees of new opportunities for innovation and creativity that can be granted to the new leader

10. The esteem a new leader will show a departing leader

11. The celebrations of success that will be part of a smooth transition

12. The quality of relationships that will let all parties know that a right successor choice was made

These intersection points serve as foundations to the building of resiliency when the baton is passed. The more intersecting points of agreement are present at the end of the day, the stronger becomes the validity of the final choice, and the more secure the future is.

Again: *Great leaders look for people who can accomplish more than the original leader.* Far from being a threat to an existing leader's position or authority, exiting leadership builds superior credibility and expands its own bearing when the new leader accomplishes more based on the original leader's model.

Living Proof: "Westin, Taylor and 'The Company Legacy'"

Westin (Wes) and Taylor ("T") had become friends in their senior year at high school and developed a friendship born not of similar backgrounds (one from wealth, the other far from it), but from some basic agreements about the value of people and a passion to achieve. Both had volunteered for community causes to help the less fortunate, and both excelled in academics and sports. They had taken similar paths of higher education but at separate institutions. Both had graduated with masters degrees, and in combination, their degrees included the disciplines of business law, business administration, management theory, psychology, and sociology.

The two reconnected after college—they wanted to work together. They matched their interests and educations and formed Wes-Taylor Industries. Both lived out their values, both were dyed-in-the-wool optimists, and both wanted to "make a difference" through Wes-Taylor and what their company could provide.

Wes-Taylor thrived, and after twenty-eight years, celebrating gross annual revenues in excess of $113 million, they mutually considered that the time was coming to create an exit strategy, although neither had a desire to retire. As they pondered their futures and the company's prospects, they learned of three leadership tracks. The principles of investment leadership were heart warming and challenging to these two businessmen. Throughout their business venture, they had certainly exercised impact and influence and had witnessed sizable corporate and profit growth result; of these facts, there was no doubt. But in looking forward to creating legacy, they understood that investment within a select few, who would be the right people for succession, was for Wes and "T," the most viable way to gain the good that would reach beyond their presence.

So their search began, first within Wes-Taylor for "rising stars" of impact, and those with positional influence already established. Both men actively used five criteria to sort out candidates and the four questions to qualify the people with the greatest potential for success. They looked for people with firmly established core values, who possessed dreams and desires, who were goal-setters and "doers," and found some! They gained permission from candidates to explore further, exercised due diligence necessary to discover degrees of experience and education, and thoroughly reviewed résumés. They outlined carefully the parameters and time lines, expectations and results. They spoke the truth openly with a focus on the welfare of the followers. In short, they proactively planned their investments for the greatest returns in building legacy and securing the company's future.

They were convinced that people were more important than production, and they also knew that production guaranteed the prospects of the company in their industry. Their actions in designing their exit strategy proved what they already believed: the value of perseverance when a right course is set, and the balance of relationship and function in people and production.

The benefits became far-reaching, as Wes and "T" concluded they would. Their successors have become success stories themselves. The new leaders are expanding on the foundation the original owners laid and are producing more.

Legacies are formed and leaders accomplish more than what they first may imagine when they invest in the right people, in the right place and time, for the right reasons.

Legacy lives when a leader who is leaving has so cultivated his or her successor that the departure contributes to exponential expansion for the organization. Legacy languishes when burdened by continued dependence upon the leader, where the leader is viewed as the singular force around whom the organization exists, and only through whom its survival is maintained.

Great leaders who build leadership rightly know and openly communicate this truth: leaving is a part of living and learning. Follower and leader welcome the opportunity for the infusion of timeless principles that timely departure opens, to help an organization survive and thrive. The passing of the baton within the investment leadership track is assured when principles of the first leader's administration are inherited, included and expanded in the second and third and fourth generations who carry on.

The goal of exiting well is successful succession. But succession, if planned and executed poorly, can introduce seeds of secession, a wholly undesirable prospect, where a company or department may suffer functional divisiveness, severed relationships, falter, or fail because its total viability has rested exclusively on the presence and visibility of a leader who has decided not to invest.

The consequences of secession are vast. Atmospheres of discontent breed disconnected actions from segmented parties who labor in distrust and disunity; at the end of the day, secession often causes complete shut down. In what could have been a flourishing environment of succession if a leader had invested, a leader who chooses not to invest will have selfishly sacrificed the futures of others who remain to pick up what's left.

There are four finish lines of success that, when crossed,

help the departing leader know if triumph is imminent and that the baton can be passed, and if quality succession will be achieved. The leader is assured that he or she is crossing these four finish lines of success, but not alone; that because of the regenerative investments and mentoring which the leader has accomplished, there are others who will finish as well, but better, in shorter time, and with more strength in reserve than the original leader's endurance and ending would allow.

Successful succession is acquired through running with a follower who is matching stride. If you are leading, it is becoming even clearer now how important your choices are as to followers, those to be mentored, to receive investments, and the techniques and tools you will use. Legacy-building requires that you proportion the resources to carry on your run in all the tracks while concentrating maximum efforts on those you believe will do greater works. The leader for legacy will pass the baton to a second generation of leaders who will pattern their runs on the model set by the original leader. When the leader's successors duplicate the original, they enthusiastically set out to find their own successors. This run is not to the swift, but to the committed and the invested from generation to generation. This run produces successful duplication and successions of enduring legacy.

The Four Finish Lines of Success

The investment leader who finishes well in any endeavor

will cross four lines of success and will do so in a sequential order. Each crossing by a leader opens the possibility of achievement for the follower right behind. One success follows another. This chronological arrangement is necessary if legacy is to be secured. Each success builds upon the one preceding it and positions success for the one proceeding after it.

These four finish lines can be used as success measurements within any enterprise. Taken in order, they will show any leader and follower in any application whether fulfillment of relationship and task, and the building of future and legacy are occurring.

In order of appearance and accomplishment they are as follows:

1. **Optimal Structure: Authority and Accountability**

    The first need is for follower and investor leader to know to whom they answer and what their roles are. Their relationship is dependent on acknowledging the authority figure, and completion of their functions relies on knowing explicitly that for which they are accountable and how they are to achieve desired results.

    Optimal structures of authority and accountability are designed and implemented by leader and follower together. To assure success in an investment leadership arrangement, this line of success must be crossed first. Your leadership responsibility is to build these structures if they don't exist; if they do, make sure they are known and obeyed.

2. **Operational Systems: Communication and Closure**

Operational systems are environments where communication and closure are customary. Optimal structures come alive when communication is effective. Together, these structures and systems provide authentic illustrations of balanced cooperation of relationship and function. Apart from operational communication and an optimal structure of authority and accountability, relationships can be reduced to mere wishes and feelings, and function with excellence seldom materializes.

The warmth of human endeavor and endurance makes structures and systems breathe. Interactive communication and closure work inside optimal structures and bring them vibrancy. Your job as the leader is to assure that communication and closure is the rule, not the exception, to promote life and succession.

Crossing this second finish line of success prepares participants for the next hands-on engagements that make or break the investment procedure seen in nurture and support. Together, nurture and support represent opportunities for selection.

3. Opportunities for Selection: Nurture and Support

Nurture and support were sketched in Chapter 5. Seen as one of the four finish lines of success that must be crossed to achieve succession, the leader evaluates and chooses which of these processes he or she will select, and at what time, for the benefit of the follower to promote maturity.

While not desiring to sit in judgment, the leader must weigh and decide what choices for assistance are needed to help a follower prepare for receiving the baton and carrying on the legacy. The leader will request permission to nurture and support the follower, and the leader assumes full responsibility for the choices and initial implementation.

The follower's responsibility is first to remember that he or she committed to the process, and that the leader has the follower's best interests at heart. Because of their mutually agreed commitments, the follower will choose receptivity to what the leader deems is needful, and they will discuss processes openly. They both entered this mentoring process with intentions of receiving and giving nurture and support, and if the time is now, they engage.

Your job as the leader is to fully explain nurture and support to the follower so that when either is applied an understanding is already in place.

Nurture is application of necessary assistance from

the outside in and is challenging when the situation calls for methods that may be uncomfortable for the follower; tough love, some would call it.

- It's when a leader takes the initiative to warn a follower from making an incorrect or negative choice that on the horizon may appear profitable but violates their agreed value system.
- It's when the leader sounds an alarm if threats that will dissuade the growth process are seen, and the temptations to break a commitment grow large.
- It's when the leader warns unequivocally of undesirable consequences should a considered negative or wrong action be taken, in breach of ethics or shirking responsibility.
- Or, it's when the leader will just plain get in the follower's face to talk sense because the leader cares and sees the follower contemplating incorrect and destructive paths.
- It's when a leader intervenes.

A nurturing invasion may not be gentle, but when needed, is undertaken because the follower is more important than what he or she is about to do.

Support is understood as actions of sharing, bearing and caring from the inside out that are welcomed in times of joy and success and moments of struggle, sadness or disappointment. Support may be more comfortable to perform than nurture, and is definitely more warmly received.

- Support is celebratory and demonstrates genuine enthusiasm when successes are achieved.
- Support is congratulatory and affirming when meritorious service is performed.
- Support is encouragement with sympathy in identification with difficult circumstances, and empathy in understanding what a follower is experiencing at the moment, to assist that follower in getting through and learning from the tough or challenging times.
- A leader picks support devices that the follower understands are uplifting. The leader knows what these are because the leader as asked about them prior to when they are needed.
- If the follower's language of receptivity is more verbal than written, conversations are employed within language types the follower appreciates. If a follower prefers more written than verbal communication, then cards, email correspondence and letters are used, again sensitive to language preferences.

Opportunities for selection of nurture and support promote the maximum and most positive long-standing effects when they proceed from carefully constructed optimal structures and operational systems of communication and closure.

Crossing these three lines of success are winning moments, and these wins are celebrated! Relationships (decisions to uphold and encourage another's success) grow stronger, and functions (acts that prove the authenticity of the decisions) are more qualitative.

Crossing the first three finish lines of success allow leader and follower to thoughtfully and energetically plan their design for crossing the final success line. Their futures are in view. Their plans for winning succession are executed, the passing of the baton is completed, and the leader's responsibilities are accomplished as desire is fulfilled in duplication.

4. **Optimistic Succession: Desire and Duplication**

Optimism is more than a wish for something positive or a way of looking at a glass with 50% content. It definitely is not a feeling. Optimism, as seen in *Leadership Is—*, is a perspective born of proof, secure in the knowledge of what works and why.

Optimism is the assurance of positive outcome in an investment leadership track because of the preparation that brought leader and follower to this position in the first place. Optimism is a guarantee, a living proof coming from attached engagement. Optimism is a certainty of outcome based on making deliberate value-system-driven choices, living in mutual understandings of vision, working hard to accomplish mission, and proclaiming the message of life-lessons the leader and follower want to communicate.

Optimism is possible because the process has been repeated and shown to be reliable over time. The process of succession succeeds whenever it is tried and faithfully executed: where the elements of success cooperate within the Code of Achievement, the Four Questions, the methods of qualification, the quality of the investment, and the realistic quantification of its outcome.

A leader and follower plan their optimistic succession and eagerly yearn to cross this fourth finish line. As they match stride in the investment leadership track, they proactively plan for when the baton is to be passed, how that event will transpire, who will see it, what the effects will be on their respective worlds, and how they will celebrate the moment. They ensure they are ready, completely ready, for this important engagement, and the results they are certain will come from it.

Optimistic succession is the product of people who combine principles, planning, and perseverance to bring a process of investment to completeness. These people understand that great leadership builds legacy and want to carry on the leadership model that has transpired and transform it into something even better to which others will aspire.

Your leadership is on the line; it may be present at the starting line, or purposed to push toward the finish: lines of success are waiting to be crossed. Your job as the leader is to prepare your people today as though you were leaving your position tomorrow, so that when tomorrow comes, they are stronger for the experience, as you will be also.

This is What Leadership Is—
Chapter 9:
Leadership's Finish: Lines of Success

Review and Reinforce:

1. The investment leadership track is a place where dreams and desires of legacies for the future are fashioned; it is also the place where finish lines of success are crossed, and the consummation of the investment brings about a living legacy and assures its future expansion.
2. A living legacy is the proof of "finishing well."
3. Business owners, entrepreneurs, and visionary leaders who have built enterprises begin at some point to look at leaving.
4. Insurance against loss is best accomplished by caring for and provisioning the people who are positioned best to carry on the enterprise and grow it once the initial or current leaders have departed.
5. Exit preparation applies to every leader who occupies any position that will include the necessity at some point to leave it.
6. If you are the leader who is investing well and preparing at some point to exit well, you consider proper exiting to be part of your desire to finish well. The expectations upon you are enormous and you need to fulfill the processes correctly.

7. A candidate to replace a leader brings relational and functional attributes that must be evaluated. These are matched with an organization's values, vision, mission and message to determine how many intersecting points exist.

8. Great leaders look for people who can accomplish more than the original leader.

9. Leaving is a part of living and learning.

10. To be assured that leadership is accomplishing its investment to build legacy and positioning to finish well, consider the four lines of success that when crossed let the leader know triumph is imminent. These are optimal structures, operational systems, opportunities for selection of nurture and support, and optimistic succession.

11. These four finish lines of success can be used as success measurements within any enterprise.

12. Your leadership is on the line. What line is it?

13. Prepare your people today as though you were leaving your position tomorrow, so that when tomorrow comes, they are stronger for the experience, as you will be also.

14. This run is not to the swift but to the committed and the invested.

10
Action Steps

"When do I have time to invest? I have a job to do." You may be contemplating or articulating this view. If so, you may not yet be ready to run on the investment track in the ways described here. But keep reading.

Every leader knows that his or her time allocation is a choice. It's one of many choices a leader makes. If investment leadership becomes a consideration, then that leader will choose the right time for the right reasons. A leader who desires more than what he or she currently has acquired will become personally responsible to set the time aside and allocate the resources to accomplish the goals that are most important. If those desires include investments in others, know now: those investments will be costly.

Let's say that you want to grow your leadership and create enduring legacy, that there are followers in your impact or influence tracks that are looking to you for more. You were introduced to the Code of Achievement in Chapter 5. Shake hands now with the Course of Attainment. The Course of Attainment will show you how to begin, what action steps to take, may provide the motives to begin, and will point up the checkpoints along the track to determine your progress as you reach out to invest in another. If you want to undertake the run in the investment leadership track, you will include the followers who want to emulate you. Using this process may help.

The Course of Attainment

The course of attainment begins with dreams, evolves into desires, is established in setting goals, and requires specific action steps in a verifiable time line to cause the dreams to become reality. Here is how the process works:

1. **Dreams**

    Don't let anyone ever steal your dream. Should someone try to convince you that your dream is not possible, you might listen respectfully to their opinions, but shun the negatives if you don't agree; change the subject, or just conclude the conversation. Your dream is yours until you give it away.

    A dream is a "what if…" perspective that imagines what could be, if…, and it is part of the gift of creativity you possess and the beliefs you hold that a condition can be better than it is. When a leader dreams, he or she is looking to the future; further, that leader knows that if the dream stays only as a dream, the future it portends will simply remain in the imagination.

Dream about your legacy and the people who will benefit because of your investment; then, if you are serious, move to desire. When you move, your follower will see it.

2. Desires

What you want is important. The third question of the Four Questions is "What do you want?" It is placed in the number three position because it has to follow the answers to question one, the question of values, and to question two, concerning vision. Your answer to this third question is brought into focus from your responses to the first two; based on your values and vision, it pointedly inquires, "What is your mission?" Your mission is what you want, the methods you will employ to achieve what you want, and the evaluations you conduct to measure your wins and losses along the way.

Until a dream of investment into a follower becomes a desire, the hunger for what can be will not replace the status of what is, and the dream will float in its dream world. But when a dream changes into a desire, the yearning of the human spirit to declare "what I want" becomes validation of your worldview (values) and your calling (vision), and a follower who wants to grow will be encouraged by your motivation.

What do you want for your leadership? Why do you want it? Does it fulfill your vision? How will you get what you want?

Desires expressed as part of the course of attainment are firmly planted when they are avowed to benefit more than just yourself; open communication to those around you, telling them what you want in fulfillment of values and vision, will encourage your accountability to your followers and lead to setting goals, your next step.

3. **Goals**

A goal defined: a purposeful objective to be reached on or before a predetermined date, the process of the conclusion of which will include specific actions within designated time lines; these time lines will be punctuated with markers for conducting evaluations, corrections, realignments, and retooling, designed to show the goal-setter at what point he or she has achieved the wins in the accomplishment of the endeavor.

When goals are set, the declaration of what is desired begins to take shape in the form of realistic expectations of return for the energy to be expended in the effort. Goals are true aims when they include precise markers of measurement of their activities and their worth as end results are achieved. Fortunately on the investment leadership track, those markers exist in abundance within the observations and conclusions your followers contribute as they see you put forth your efforts.

Goal setting is not a timid activity; it is an out-in-the-open tenacious fixing of energy and action into an exact time frame in which success or failure will be known. A leader who is serious about investing will set these aims and follow them with action.

4. **Action Steps**

Action steps are the specific and sequential activities in real life that lead to the fulfillment of a goal. Each step may stand alone, but all the steps are inter-related to form a composite of accomplishment. Each should be planned, each should be measured, and all should be completed. Evaluation of actions should show that each step has exceeded the expectation of results associated with it, where former lines of excellence have become new lines of mediocrity.

The title of this chapter is "Action Steps." Upon finishing up the book, you will determine as you evaluate if anything you have read here has encouraged you to consider changes in your conduct in becoming a leader and growing in your leadership effectiveness. If so, you will know that the lessons here will have stuck, if, and only if, you act. Any action steps you decide to take will be evidenced only in behavioral changes, will be shown in measurable movement, and will provide further motivation toward the realization of your dreams. Without action steps, words of declared decisions are void of power; with them, words of commitment are validated in observable measures because behavioral changes produce consequences.

Committing to action steps pushes character to demonstrate its real constitution. And this is the rub. Characteristics of giving up or faithfully committing—both are born in very early stages of learning and show whether an individual accepts personal responsibility and ownership of solutions to life's situations, or shirks accountability, deferring initiative to someone else. Effects of these early choices can last a lifetime and become frameworks into which all challenges are put: either to be met head-on with cause or excused and swept away.

Let's say you decide to lead and build a legacy according to the model presented in *Leadership Is—*. You commit to turning a dream of leadership into a desire and set your goals. You initiate your action. What will determine your confidence level to proceed when the negatives appear? Will giving up or faithfulness be what your followers see?

When fulfilling an investment commitment gets down right hard, true character comes to the forefront. It shows determination in meeting challenges or dissolution in melting before them. If you want to be an effective leader whose legacy lasts, your dedication to the process of action is required, regardless of circumstances.

Investment will not happen "on its own." You must take the initiative. Fortunately for a person who has practiced mere wishful thinking, non-commitment, or lack of faithfulness, it is possible to make the choices to live in trustworthy and verifiable character at any time; if your dreams are big enough, your desires strong enough, and your goals clear enough—again, these are all choices the individual makes. If your desire is legacy leadership, you will make these choices.

An investment leader's committed actions form the evidence of how willing a leader is to follow-through on his or her commitments. This is the model that teaches the follower how to follow before teaching the follower how to lead.

Action steps are more than lists of a leader's assignments; they are proving grounds of reliability and faithfulness. Within their engagement, true tests of character are conducted: the context of the values and vision is verified by the content of the mission if fulfilled; and the message of the strength of relationship is validated by the function or discredited in its failure.

No dream becomes possible without desire. No desire becomes probable apart from goals. No goal becomes accomplished without action steps. Your actions as the investor leader show the strength of your commitment to create a "greater works" opportunity for your follower, as you and the follower match stride in the investment leadership track.

5. **Reality**

Reality is the passing of the baton (the code of achievement embraced and engaged into another's experience). Reality marks the moment when an investment leader's actions are completed within the time line that was decided, the four finish lines have been crossed, the leader's model is emulated by the follower, and the celebrations for the accomplishment of the follower becoming the leader are enjoyed to the max.

Reality is when relationships have been corroborated in function, and an original leader "leaves" to begin another investment when the opportunity is right. Reality is when the former follower has been best positioned for "greater works" than the original leader.

Reality is when the legacy is living, and the lessons learned are embedded into the life experiences of the new leader. Reality is when the new leader begins his or her process of investing into lives of followers by running in the same track, fulfilling the course of attainment.

Reality is not a final destination; it's a moment of new determination to initiate the process all over again. Leaders running in the investment track are insatiable in their desires and efforts for growth and development in others. They continually anticipate and work toward the moments when the baton will be passed again. While they may become tired because of effort they expend, they are never retired from starting the engagement again.

Remember what leadership is— it is a state of interaction with others that can and must be cultivated to create duplicative results for positive and regenerating impact.

Reality expects greater works as behaviors change and investments grow. Leaders encourage and promote their followers to anticipate and achieve more. The realistic expectations for exponential results represent unquenchable yearnings from leaders whose passion is to invest in others lives to make a difference.

This is What Leadership Is —
Chapter 10:
Action Steps

Review and Reinforce:

1. Time allocation is a choice.
2. A leader who desires more than what he or she currently has acquired will become personally responsible to set the time aside and allocate the resources to accomplish the goals that are most important. If those desires include investments in others, know now: those investments will be costly.
3. If you want to undertake the run in the investment leadership track, you will include the followers who want to emulate you, and use the Course of Attainment.
4. The Course of Attainment: dreams, desires, goals, action steps, reality.
5. Your dream is yours until you give it away.
6. When a leader dreams, he or she is looking to the future; further, that leader knows that if the dream stays only as a dream, the future it portends will simply remain in the imagination.
7. When your dream changes into a desire, the yearning of the human spirit to declare "what I want" becomes validation of your world-view (values) and your

calling (vision), and a follower who wants to grow will be encouraged by your motivation.

8. Goal setting is not a timid activity; it is an out-in-the-open tenacious fixing of energy and action into an exact time frame in which success or failure will be known.

9. Action steps are the specific and sequential activities in real life that lead to the fulfillment of a goal.

10. Words of commitment are validated in observable measures because behavioral changes produce consequences.

11. Committing to action steps pushes character to demonstrate its real constitution.

12. Action steps are more than lists of a leader's duties; they are the proving grounds of reliability and faithfulness.

13. Reality is not a final destination; it's a moment of new determination to initiate the process all over again.

14. Reality expects greater works as behaviors change and investments grow.

Summary

A leader in the design of *Leadership Is—* possesses characteristics of ethics, morals, behaviors, and accountability that set him or her apart from others who may wear the badge but not embrace the responsibility. A leader in this design desires life improvement.

Three leadership tracks and traits help a leader understand positions and expectations of leaders and followers within the tracks that are chosen: impact leadership and its relationships of dependence; influence leadership and its relationships of independence; and investment leadership and its relationships of inter-dependence.

Each track has its own merits; running in one does not compete with running in another; rather, a complete understanding of broadened leadership responsibilities will probably include a leader's running in all three tracks simultaneously. A leader chooses the tracks and expends the energy according to the desired results and agreements of the leader and follower.

A leader who seeks to build legacy looks for followers who desire to move into the investment leadership track, where the investor leader takes the initiative. It is here where the passing of a baton of living legacy is accomplished.

The leader qualifies him or herself and the follower who wants to receive the leader's investments, determining if follower and leader are ready for this run. Upon passing the qualifying trials and within mutual agreement, they begin this run together, matching stride.

During the run, the investment leader spends dedicated time, energy and resources in providing quality investments in a predetermined time line that has specific start and end dates. They adhere to the Code of Achievement. This code is made up of the values, vision, mission and message of an enterprise and becomes the character of the baton to be passed. Positions of authority and accountability are properly established. Relational investment will include use of the Four Questions to open discussions about personal growth. Functional responsibility, open lines of communication, cooperative problem solving and conflict resolution, and creating realistic expectations of the results are integrated elements of the quality investments a leader provides.

The quality of the investment is weighed as its processes go through quantifying tests. Evaluations are not optional. Motives and methods of correction and readjustment are applied, and leader and follower enjoy the celebrations of wins. They anticipate their next steps and engage in future planning.

Creating leadership models that work is accomplished when a leader finishes well. A value system provides a grid of measurement to ascertain degrees of alignment with standards that have stood the tests of trial through time. The Twelve Laws of Understanding provides a sample value system. A value system should be compared to the nine proofs of abiding results that showcase proven reliability. Integrating a value system into real life is best accomplished through mentoring.

Leaders in the design of *Leadership Is—* want to move the people who desire it into greater growth and productivity. The preferred and recommended tools a leader will employ are motivation and deputizing. A leader will reject manipulation and delegation. People are treasures, and because they are more important than what they do, they are treated as the most valuable and therefore the most valued resources any organization possesses.

Investment leaders look to points of exit and understand that leaving is a part of living and learning. Leadership is finished when it crosses four finish lines of success: those of optimal structure, operational systems, opportunities for selection of nurture and support, and optimistic succession. Leaders look for followers who will produce greater works than the original leader perhaps ever even imagined.

Investment leaders who want to turn their leadership investment dreams into reality in the life of a follower will use the Course of Attainment. The Course of Attainment: dreams, desires, goals, action steps, and reality. When dreams become reality, the process begins again, and expects exponential results.

A leader in the design of *Leadership Is—* becomes a living proof of the results of building a legacy that lasts.

Action Steps for You, the Investment Leader

1. Qualify yourself by evaluating your character. What kind of core do you have?
2. Decide how your leadership is positioned within your networks; know the tracks on which you are running now.
3. What baton will you pass? What makes up your Code of Achievement? How do you answer the Four Questions? Know what is important to you that should live in your legacy.
4. Engage in qualifying trials with followers who want to grow through your expanded investment.
5. Upon passing these trials and gaining agreement between you and your follower, generate quality investments.
6. Employ quantifying tests to evaluate your investments and to measure progress.
7. Create a value system based on the nine proofs that have stood the tests of trial through time.
8. Move your committed follower through motivation and deputizing.

9. Cross the four finish lines of success with your follower; pass the baton.

10. Use the Course of Attainment to turn your investment dreams into reality.

Conclusion

Effective leadership is costly over time, but in the right time and in the right places with the right people, sees great rewards. One of those rewards is realized when the follower begins to demonstrate transferable leadership characteristics, molded and modeled from his or her leader, seeking a follower of his or her own into whom to invest. The process works and becomes duplicative, beginning all over again as follower-apprentice becomes leader-mentor.

The three tracks of leadership are always occupied; choosing the right ones for you and the people who look to you for leadership will determine the quality of the legacy you leave and your succession's success. Choose well.

Start. Set a date. Follow through. Continue. Lead.
Build legacy. Celebrate.

Leadership Is—
how to build your legacy. The baton will be passed.

Leadership Is—
a sentence that you complete. It will emerge from the
values and characteristics you embrace.

Leadership Is—
a business-life investment model. It will benefit your
business today and prepare it to thrive tomorrow.

Leadership Is—
a business life-investment model. It will change the
lives it touches because it changes behaviors.

Leadership Is—
a choice you make. It will live through you and beyond
you in the contributions of those who you prepare
to accomplish greater works.

Within the process of investment leadership, lives are
touched with truth coming from authenticity of character,
expressed from integrity at the heart of the leader, and a
proven dedication to helping someone else achieve success. If
you're the leader, you are invited to consider the opportunities
that *Leadership Is—* presents. All choices have consequences,
so consider your choices carefully, and then act upon them.

Perhaps, as you contemplate this leadership model of timeless principles, you will choose to build your legacy by completing it through timely application. Your response to participate is welcomed. Your choices will change you and the ones you lead. Indeed, your legacy will live in this truth: *Lead well, and build people for life.*

Twelve Laws of Understanding

1. Realize I am responsible for my own choices, not others'; that changing someone else's behavior is not my responsibility; rather, I need to change me.
2. Seek to understand how the other person thinks and communicates; use his or her language.
3. Model what I want.
4. Set realistic limits on what is acceptable behavior.
5. Impose these limits on myself, first.
6. Desire the best, but prepare for difficulty; seek creative, peaceful solutions.
7. Seek and pray for wisdom.
8. Remember, at the right times.
9. Encourage always.
10. Think first, listen most, and speak seldom.
11. Realize growth involves change, change can mean pain, and patience on the journey is a virtue.
12. Love. Establish meaningful relationships.

C reative
T eam
R esources
G roup

Creative Team Resources Group (CTRG, www.ctrg.com) provides quality resources for the development of teams within organizations whose desires are to grow and develop their personnel and achieve greater results in product or service provision. CTRG gives people great information that allows them to make changes in how they live and work and does this through building core teams. Our resources include conferences, consultation and coaching.

Our foundational principle is that people are more important than production and relationships precede and give definition to function. The value of a person's contributions comes from that person's inherent worth. The value of the person causes the contributions a person makes to achieve even greater results.

Contact CTRG. We will demonstrate first-hand how our team building principles can work for you. Glen Aubrey,

President and CEO, along with other CTRG staff are available to your group for speaking engagements, on-site training and leadership coaching. CTRG looks forward to serving and working with you!

Acknowledgements

A lifetime of a family's love and teaching, examples of faith and belief, a treasure trove of enduring friendships, thousands of authors, educators, musicians and multi-faceted creative artisans, along with inspiring and challenging contemporary and historical leaders, mentors, speakers and business associates have helped to shape the foundations and bring the principles and practices illustrated in this book to life. To thank them all by listing each would be an impossible task, but I am grateful for the countless life-investing influence and encouragement given to me.

I offer special appreciation to those who have been vitally and eminently important in the activities involved in the creation of this work, and without whom the book would simply not have been possible.

Special thanks to:

Cindy Aubrey, my wife, the mother of our children, whom I honor for her support, a singer of remarkable ability, with whom I share the joy of our grandchildren.

Heather Aubrey, my daughter, whom I love dearly and who never fails to make me laugh, who has a passion for helping maturing young ladies find and walk in faith, who has worked in administration for our company, Creative Team Resources Group (CTRG).

Justin Aubrey, my son, in whom I am indeed well pleased, a fast-developing and extremely talented professional artist, brilliant thinker, a young man of high values and quick wit with fewer but so well-placed words, the designer of the book's original cover concept, my buddy whose smile never fails to warm my heart, and whose presence brings us great joy.

"Mom" Aubrey, my mother, who at this writing (2004) is 88 years young, an earnestly dedicated student and vibrant teacher, a cheerleader and confidence giver throughout my life who provides her genuine support in prayer and encouragement nearly every time we talk, whose desires to learn and grow serve as an inspiration to many in addition to her son.

My father, "Bud" Aubrey, who died in 1982, whose support of my early efforts at communication in music and speech set a stage of assurance and belief I deeply appreciate, a solid business leader in his own right whom I know would be pleased with this offering but whose greatest joy would undoubtedly be our extended family, and especially his grandchildren and great grandchildren.

Jeff Goble, one of my close associates in CTRG, my "right arm" in computer technology, a solid contributor in analysis, document design and trouble-shooting, a deep and innovative thinker and writer from whom I continually learn, and one with whom I gratefully share mutual investments of time, enterprise, energy and humor.

Hayley Beck, one of our CTRG support team members, my book editor, who hails from Australia, possesses a delightful and contagious view of the world, a wonderful friend who along with her husband, Randy, inspires integrity and faithfulness, who has my abiding trust and respect, plus, she's unbelievably fast on the computer.

Katherine Michaud, our first Acquisitions Editor and Book Editor, whose attention to detail, timely responses to multiple questions and thoughtful encouragement have assisted us in the publication process, contributing not only her efforts but her enthusiasm for this work, who is an accomplished poet in her own right, and has helped us begin and complete this important goal.

Jordan Trementozzi, who is like another daughter to me, whose writing and book editing talents never cease to amaze me, who with her husband, Chris, contribute time and talents to ongoing Creative Team Resources Group (CTRG) and Creative Team Publishing (CTP) projects, fulfilling their responsibilities with excellence.